1988 Mutual Fund

Fact Book

Industry trends and statistics for 1987

Investment
Company
Institute

145440
G

Table of Contents

How to Use This Book

The *1988 Mutual Fund Fact Book* is a basic guide to the trends and statistics that were observed and recorded during the year of 1987.

Text and Data. The Fact Book is divided into two main sections—text and data. A glossary appears at the end of the text section.

The first part of the book—text—covers basics in the history and development of the industry, key benefits and features of mutual funds, and 1987 trends in mutual funds. A series of charts, graphs, and tables illustrate some of the latest trends and help the reader compare 1987 to prior years' activity. To locate specific charts, graphs, and tables found in the text portion of the book, refer to the index on page 107.

The data section (the green pages) begins with its own table of contents to make it easy to find the specific information needed. Each table in this section is clearly labeled by classification, for example, Industry Totals, Long-Term Funds, Short-Term Funds, etc. If you cannot find the data you need in the data table of contents, again, please refer to the index on page 107.

Data Classification. As you use the Fact Book, keep in mind that the industry usually divides its statistics into two broad categories: long-term funds (stock, bond, and income funds) and short-term funds (money market and short-term municipal bond funds). To obtain the total industry picture, refer to the notes at the bottom of the tables in both the text and the data sec-

tions (the green pages). In the Long-Term Funds section, for example, a note at the bottom of the page will refer to comparable short-term data or total industry data, when applicable.

The portion of the data section containing total industry statistics is a recent addition to the Fact Book. It includes information on total industry shareholder accounts, assets, and number of funds. (This section does not provide total sales figures which would combine long-term and short-term fund sales. Due to the special nature of short-term funds and the huge, continuous inflows and outflows of money they experience, it would be misleading to add their sales figures to those of the long-term funds. Tracking periodic changes in total assets is usually the preferred method of following trends of short-term funds.)

Beginning with this year's Fact Book, the Institute has further refined the industry's investment objectives by adding seven categories. The new categories are global equity, global bond, flexible portfolio, high-yield bond, income-equity, income-bond, and short-term state municipal bond—bringing the total number of fund categories to 22.

These categories have been recalculated back to 1984, so all tables involving data broken down by investment objective include only 1984, 1985, 1986, and 1987. (Prior to this year's edition, the data for these categories were included in a variety of the 15 already existing categories.)

1

1987: The Beginnings of Change

The U.S. economy began to show signs of change in 1987 even though the expansion continued for its fifth straight year. The economy grew at a rate of 4 percent for the year, but this respectable advance was not totally convincing to the financial markets. Both the bond and stock markets experienced substantial price setbacks during the year, which led to lower investor demand for funds and a reappraisal by many of their investment strategies.

Signs of economic change are evident in the components of GNP. Unlike economic growth in the earlier years of the expansion, 1987's advances were not as dependent upon personal consumption expenditures. A sharp decline in the value of the dollar as compared to major foreign currencies helped to improve real net exports. The improvement in real net exports—$21 billion for 1987—was the first since 1980 and was especially important in spurring fixed investments by businesses.

Meanwhile, personal spending was slowed by relatively modest gains in real disposable income and the effects of the stock market drop in the latter part of the year. Consumers may have responded to market uncertainty by cutting back on their spending and increasing savings.

Inflation increased in 1987 over the previous year's level. The consumer price index for all urban consumers (CPI-U) rose by 4.4 percent as compared to 1.1 percent in 1986. Most of this increase can be attributed to oil prices. Higher short- and long-term interest rates accompanied the upward movement of prices. Interest rates generally climbed during the year except for a short period in midsummer and at yearend.

Inflationary expectations, however, were only part of the interest rate story. The growing weakness of the dollar was a strong contributor to the changed interest rate environment of 1987. When trade figures reacted less than expected to the dollar's decline, uncertainty surrounding the prospects of private (i.e., largely foreign) demand for U.S. government securities mounted. The Federal Reserve (the Fed) responded by tightening credit during the first part of the year. This less accommodating monetary policy was adjusted in the second half of 1987 as changing economic and financial conditions emerged.

The Fed was faced with a major turning point in October. After climbing steadily (and sometimes dramatically) over much of the year, stock prices, as measured by the S&P 500 index, abruptly fell. During the last quarter of 1987, stock prices dropped by 22.5 percent to close the year only slightly higher than where they began. Bond prices were hit earlier in the year when interest rates advanced, but recovered after the stock market's troubles began.

Mutual fund sales reacted quickly to the changed market climate. Sales of both stock funds and bond funds peaked during the first four months of 1987 and then declined for the rest of the year. Bond and income funds were particularly affected. Sales of these funds totaled about $66.0 billion through April, as compared to $52.6 billion for the remainder of the year.

The decline was less dramatic for stock funds—at least until October—

Interest Rates

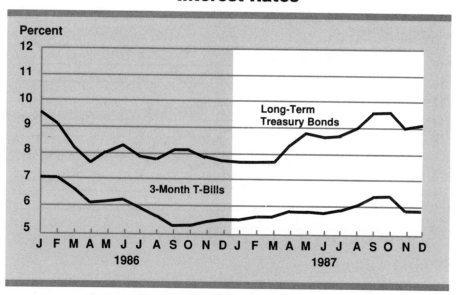

Stock Prices

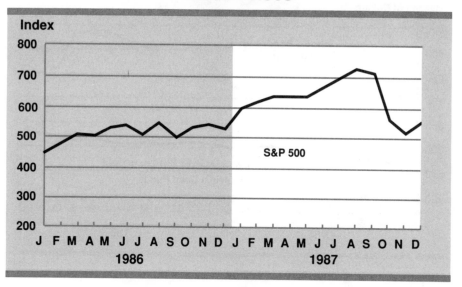

with $31.7 billion in sales through April and $40.4 billion for the last eight months of 1987. In spite of this slowing, stock funds outsold 1986 lev-els by $14.4 billion ($72.1 billion as compared to $57.7 billion). Bond and income fund sales lagged the previous year's level by $39.5 billion ($118.6 bil-

3

Mutual Fund Sales

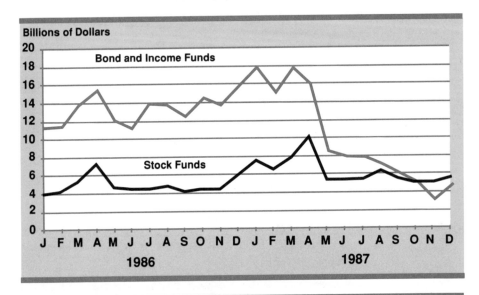

Billions of Dollars

Bond and Income Funds

Stock Funds

J F M A M J J A S O N D J F M A M J J A S O N D
1986   1987

Mutual Fund Total Net Assets

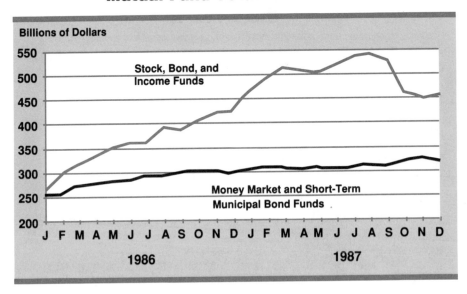

Billions of Dollars

Stock, Bond, and
Income Funds

Money Market and Short-Term
Municipal Bond Funds

J F M A M J J A S O N D J F M A M J J A S O N D
1986   1987

lion versus $158.1 billion).

Total sales of aggressive growth, growth, growth and income, precious metals, international, global equity, income-equity, flexible portfolio, and global bond funds each increased in 1987. These increases, however, were overshadowed by sales declines in all other categories of funds. Bond and income fund sales fell more rapidly

4

than sales of other types of funds. Specifically, sales of U.S. Government, Ginnie Mae, and municipal bond funds—the funds that were in the forefront of the sales boom of 1985 and 1986—also led on the way down. These same groups of funds ranked at the top in terms of outright redemptions and net exchanges out of funds in 1987.

With total sales of long-term funds down and redemptions up—total redemptions for long-term funds almost doubled for the year—net sales turned negative for a short period in 1987 after more than three years of record increases. In 1985 and 1986, net sales of stock funds and bond and income funds amounted to $81 billion and $149 billion, respectively. Investors channeled an additional $74 billion into these funds in 1987, but the pattern of flow changed markedly over the course of the year.

In the first half of 1987, net sales amounted to $70.7 billion, compared to only $3.8 billion during the balance of the year. Investors in 1987 clearly began redirecting their investments from stock, bond, and income funds to other types of financial products, such as money market funds.

The turnaround in net sales combined with slowing price appreciation to affect the growth of fund assets in 1987. Fund assets continued to grow but at a more modest pace than in 1986. Stock fund assets grew to over $180 billion and bond and income fund assets grew to almost $273 billion.

Short-term fund assets rose for the year, but also at a slower rate than in 1986. Total short-term fund assets reached $316.1 billion in 1987. Declining stock and bond prices had a definite impact on short-term fund assets, especially during the latter part of the year. Most of the increase in money market fund assets reflect exchanges out of equity and debt-oriented funds within a complex. This suggests that money market funds are performing their functions of providing investors with safety and liquidity.

Mutual Funds Net New Money Flow Related to Net New Money Flow From Individuals to Savings and Investment Vehicles

(Billions of Dollars)

Year	Net New Money to Savings and Investment Vehicles[1]	Net New Money to Mutual Funds[2]	Mutual Funds Net New Money as a Percent of Total
1960	$ 32.5	$ 1.3	4.0%
1965	59.0	2.4	4.1
1970	78.8	1.6	2.0
1975	174.4	0.5	0.3
1980	326.3	31.4	9.6
1981	353.2	109.6	31.0
1982	402.3	37.6	9.3
1983	502.6R	(18.2)	—
1984	573.8R	73.0	12.7R
1985	565.5R	88.9	15.7R
1986	538.7R	190.0	35.3R
1987	434.2	72.8	16.8

[1]From the "FRB Study of the Volume and Composition of Individuals' Savings" as reported in the Statistical Bulletins. Seasonally adjusted annual rates of individuals' savings.
[2]Investment Company Institute reporting companies, including money market funds.
R—Revised

What Is a Mutual Fund?

The Basics

A mutual fund is a company that makes investments on behalf of individuals and institutions with similar financial goals.

Pooling is the key to mutual fund investing. By pooling the financial resources of thousands of shareholders—each with a different amount to invest—investors gain access to the expertise of the country's top money managers, wide diversification of ownership in the securities markets, and a variety of services otherwise available only to institutions and wealthy families and individuals.

Professional money managers take this pool of money and invest it in a variety of stocks, bonds, or other securities selected from a broad range of industries and government agencies and authorities. Money managers select securities that best meet their fund's investment objectives. These managers make the decisions on when to buy, when to sell, and when to hold based on their extensive research.

The investment objective set forth by the fund is important to both the manager and the investor. The fund manager uses it as a guide when choosing investments for the fund's portfolio. Investors use it to determine which funds are suitable for their needs. Mutual funds' investment objectives cover a wide range, from higher risk in the search for higher returns to immediate income from more stable investments. The Investment Company Institute classifies mutual funds into 22 major categories of investment objectives. (For a definition of each, see pages 8–9.)

To achieve these objectives, fund managers may invest in as many as 50 to 200 or more different securities, seeking diversification among companies, industries, and other organizations and institutions in order to reduce investment risk. The object: to avoid putting all one's investment eggs in one basket. In effect, each investor within the fund owns a proportionate share of each of those securities. When those securities appreciate in value—or pay out dividends or interest—all the fund's investors reap their proportionate share. Investors who put $1,000 into the fund get the same rate of return or yield as those putting in $100,000.

Mutual funds can make money for their shareholders in three ways. One, they pay shareholders dividends and interest earned from the fund's investments. Two, if a security held by a fund is sold at a profit, funds pay shareholders capital gains distributions. And three, if the value of the securities held by the fund increases, the value of each mutual fund share increases proportionately.

For example, if a fund's investment objective is current income, it will invest in stocks or bonds which produce current dividends or interest. Then the fund passes through to its shareholders the dividends from those earnings.

Capital gains are realized when a fund sells a security for a higher price than it originally paid. The fund usually passes that gain through to its shareholders as a capital gains distribution. (If the gain is not passed along, investors profit from an increased value of their fund shares.)

Shareholders can have dividends and capital gains reinvested in additional shares of the fund or they can have the

6

fund send them a check for the amount of earnings.

If the securities held in the fund's portfolio increase in value, but the fund holds on to those securities instead of selling them, this increases the value of the fund's total portfolio and thus the fund's price per share.

When investors pool their money in a mutual fund, their dollars buy shares in that fund. To determine the price of these shares, at the end of each business day the fund adds up the value of all securities held in its portfolio and divides the total by the number of shares outstanding. Unlike a traditional corporation, mutual funds can issue an unlimited number of shares. In addition, shareholders have the right to redeem part or all of their holdings at any time.

Each day, the fund must determine both the value of its portfolio and how many shares are outstanding. That simple calculation gives the fund its Net Asset Value or NAV. Because it represents the value of a single share in the fund, the NAV is important to know when the fund shareholder is either redeeming shares or purchasing new shares.

To determine the value of their holdings, individual fund shareholders simply multiply the number of shares they own by the NAV. Although the NAV may not seem to change much over time, dividend and capital gain reinvestments can contribute toward buying many more shares than originally purchased. So even if the price of each share does not change a great deal, owning many more of them represents an increase in the value of the shareholder's investment.

Under the Internal Revenue Code, mutual funds that observe certain guidelines serve as conduits through which the capital gains, dividends, interest, and other income flow through from the securities held in the fund's portfolio to the shareholders. Ordinarily, mutual funds pay no tax on this income. Instead, individual shareholders treat dividends and capital gains received from the fund exactly as they would had they bought and sold the securities themselves without the fund serving as an intermediary.

For tax purposes, shareholders receive a yearend statement from the fund showing clearly what part of the money distributed to them represents ordinary income and what part represents long-term capital gains. (Even though dividends and long-term capital gains are taxed the same under the Tax Reform Act of 1986, the distinction between them is maintained since capital gains can still be offset by capital losses.) Shareholders also receive regular statements from the fund that not only show them how their investments are doing, but also report on the fund's progress, its portfolio holdings, expenses, changes in management, and other relevant data.

How a Fund Is Organized

A management company may offer anywhere from one mutual fund to a dozen or more, each with a different investment objective.

When a new fund is established, it enters into a contract with an investment adviser (usually the sponsoring organization) to manage the fund and to select its portfolio. The investment adviser is usually paid for these services through a fee based on the total value of assets managed. Such investment management fees average about one-half of one percent annually. Other fund operating expenses are usually in the same range, for a total of about one percent per year for all the fund's costs of operations.

Funds may also contract with a principal underwriter who arranges for the distribution of the fund's shares to the investing public.

Fund shares are distributed to the public in a variety of ways. There are two basic avenues, however: funds that market their shares directly to the public and those that market their shares through a sales force. Funds that market shares directly often use advertising and direct mail to reach investors. Their shares are usually distributed with low or no sales commission. In some cases, the fund's directors may authorize use of a small percentage of fund assets to support distribution efforts.

Fund shares marketed through a sales force are available through brokers, financial planners, insurance agents, and, in some cases, through a sales force employed by a fund organization specifically to market the shares of its associated funds. These sales people can be compensated for their services to the investor through a direct sales commission included in the price at which the fund's shares are offered, through a distribution fee paid by the fund, or in both ways.

All mutual fund activities are highly regulated. Mutual funds must register with the United States Securities and Exchange Commission pursuant to the Investment Company Act of 1940. The activities of mutual funds and their relationship with the public are regulated under this and other federal securities laws, as well as the securities laws of all the states where securities are sold. (See the "Regulation and Taxation" chapter.)

Types of Mutual Funds

Aggressive Growth Funds seek maximum capital gains as their investment objective. Current income is not a significant factor. Some may invest in stocks that are somewhat out of the mainstream, such as those in fledgling companies, new industries, companies fallen on hard times, or industries temporarily out of favor. They may also use specialized investment techniques such as option writing. The risks are obvious, but the potential for reward should also be greater.

Growth Funds invest in the common stock of more settled companies, but again, the primary aim is to produce an increase in the value of their investments through capital gains, rather than a steady flow of dividends.

Growth and Income Funds invest mainly in the common stock of companies with a longer track record—companies that have both the expectation of a higher share value and a solid record of paying dividends.

Precious Metals Funds invest in the stocks of gold mining companies and other companies in the precious metals business.

International Funds invest in the stocks of companies located outside the U.S.

Global Equity Funds invest in the stocks of both U.S. companies and foreign companies.

Income-Equity Funds invest primarily in stocks of companies with good dividend-paying records.

Option/Income Funds seek a high current return by investing primarily in dividend-paying common stocks on which call options are traded on national securities exchanges. Current return generally consists of dividends, premiums from writing call options, net short-term gains from sales of portfolio securities on exercises of options or otherwise, and any profits from closing purchase transactions.

Flexible Portfolio Funds invest in common stocks, bonds, money market securities, and other types of debt securities. The portfolio may

(Continued on next page)

8

Types of Mutual Funds *(Continued)*

hold up to 100 percent of any one of these types of securities or any combination thereof, and may easily change depending upon market conditions.

Global Bond Funds invest in bonds issued by companies or countries worldwide, including the U.S.

Balanced Funds generally have a three-part investment objective: 1) to conserve the investors' principal; 2) to pay current income; and 3) to increase both principal and income. They aim to achieve this by owning a mixture of bonds, preferred stocks, and common stocks.

Income-Mixed Funds seek a high level of current income for their shareholders. This may be achieved by investing in the common stock of companies that have good dividend-paying records. Often corporate and government bonds are also part of the portfolio.

Income-Bond Funds invest in a combination of government and corporate bonds for the generation of income.

U.S. Government Income Funds invest in a variety of government securities. These include U.S. Treasury bonds, federally guaranteed mortgage-backed securities, and other government issues.

GNMA or Ginnie Mae Funds (Government National Mortgage Association) invest in government-backed mortgage securities. To qualify for this category, the majority of the portfolio must always be invested in mortgage-backed securities.

Corporate Bond Funds, like income funds, seek a high level of income. They do so by buying bonds of corporations for the majority of the fund's portfolio. The rest of the portfolio may be in U.S. Treasury and other government entities' bonds.

High-Yield Bond Funds are corporate bond funds that predomi-

nantly invest in bonds rated below investment grade. In return for a generally higher yield, investors bear a greater degree of risk than for more highly rated bonds.

Long-Term Municipal Bond Funds invest in bonds issued by local governments—such as cities and states—which use the money to build schools, highways, libraries and the like. These funds predominantly invest at all times in municipal bonds that are exempt from federal income tax. Because the federal government does not tax the income earned on most of these securities, the fund can pass the tax-free income through to shareholders.

Long-Term State Municipal Bond Funds predominantly invest at all times in municipal bonds which are exempt from federal income tax as well as exempt from state taxes for residents of the state specified by the fund name.

Short-Term National Municipal Bond Funds invest in municipal securities with relatively short maturities. They are also known as tax-exempt money market funds.

Short-Term State Municipal Bond Funds invest in municipal securities with relatively short maturities. Because they contain the issues of only one state, they are exempt from state taxes for residents of the state specified by the fund name.

Money Market Mutual Funds invest in the short-term securities sold in the money market. (Large companies, banks, and other institutions invest their surplus cash in the money market for short periods of time.) In the entire investment spectrum, these are generally the safest, most stable securities available. They include Treasury Bills, certificates of deposit of large banks, and commercial paper (the short-term IOUs of large U.S. corporations).

Historical Background

America's mutual fund industry has enjoyed enormous success since the first fund was organized in Boston in 1924.

That fund, and the profusion of funds to follow, were an outgrowth of a concept originating in nineteenth century England. Later in the century, money invested in English and Scottish investment companies (or trusts, as they are known there) contributed to the financing of the American economy after the Civil War. Investors in these British companies financed U.S. farm mortgages, railroads, and other industries.

In the early 1920s, as twentieth century America began to mature, many types of financial institutions were formed, offering Americans wider avenues for investment. Several companies, most of them located in New York, Boston, and Philadelphia, tried to meet those needs. Soon, these bankers, brokers, and investment counselors were joined by mutual funds.

Shortly after the first funds were organized, America witnessed the stock market crash of 1929. Despite setbacks, many of the efficiently managed investment companies maintained their pattern of growth and service, and the industry has grown dramatically over the years.

In 1936, under a Congressional mandate, the Securities and Exchange Commission (SEC) undertook a special study of investment companies which culminated in the Investment Company Act of 1940. Industry professionals who worked closely with the SEC to draft the 1940 act decided to form a permanent committee to cooperate with the SEC in formulating the rules and regulations that would implement the new law. The committee would also stay informed of trends in state and federal legislation affecting mutual funds. This pioneering committee would be called the National Committee of Investment Companies.

As their activities increased, the committee leadership decided in October 1941 to change the organization's name to the National Association of Investment Companies (NAIC). NAIC, based in New York City, took on the responsibilities of public education, liaison with the SEC, the monitoring of tax and other legislation affecting mutual funds, as well as exerting a strong influence to maintain high industry standards. NAIC changed its name to the Investment Company Institute (ICI) in 1961. In 1970, ICI moved to Washington, DC.

The industry ICI represents has undergone many changes since the 1940 legislation which gave it birth. At that time, there were only 68 mutual funds with $448 million in assets and 296,000 shareholder accounts. It was an industry primarily providing a way to invest in the stock market. Some funds invested in bonds, but these were not a significant force until many years later.

The industry progressed steadily until the 1970s. By then, there were 400 funds with assets of about $40 billion. In the early 1970s, a new concept signaled a dramatic change in the industry—the money market mutual fund. This novel concept let the small investor participate in the high short-term interest rates of the money market that previously were available only to major institutions and the wealthy.

The idea cracked the mold in many respects. First, new investors who had never been in mutual funds gave money market funds a try. Some had never had their money in anything but 5¼ or 5½ percent passbook accounts. Many learned the value of the mutual fund concept and, in fact, 30 percent of all mutual fund investors say their first fund was a money market fund.

Second, the money market funds sparked a surge of creativity in the industry. What followed were municipal bond funds in 1976 (achieved in the enactment of the Tax Reform Act of 1976), option/income funds in 1977, government income and Ginnie Mae funds in the early 1980s, and specialty or sector funds throughout that period. At the end of 1987, there were more than 2,300 mutual funds with assets of more than $769 billion. The industry continues to grow and prosper despite periods of market volatility, providing investment diversification and professional management to over 28 million individual investors.

11

Growth and Development

The mutual fund industry is now a diversified financial industry able to respond to varied investment climates and investor needs. That was not always the case. Ten years ago, money market funds accounted for only 8.0 percent of mutual fund assets. At the same time, equity (stock) funds held 61.2 percent of the assets.

By 1980, that had changed. Money market funds (combined with their new tax-exempt version—short-term municipal bond funds) comprised 57 percent of all mutual fund assets. Equity funds represented 30 percent of assets and bond and income funds had only 13 percent. In 1987, bond and income funds had a bigger share than equity funds: 35.5 percent versus 23.5 percent. Meanwhile, short-term funds (money market and short-term municipals) made up less than half of all assets— standing at 41.0 percent at yearend 1987. This continued shifting of assets indicates widespread investor acceptance of the variety of mutual fund portfolios now offered by the industry.

Total assets have skyrocketed in these eight short years. Money market fund assets have jumped from $74.5 bil-

Percent Distribution of Total Net Assets By Type of Fund

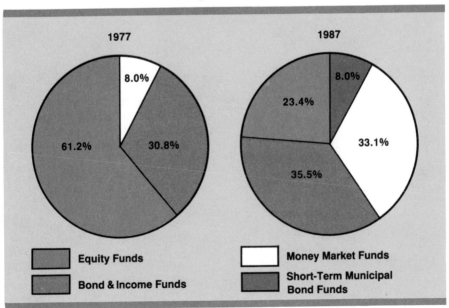

Number of Mutual Funds

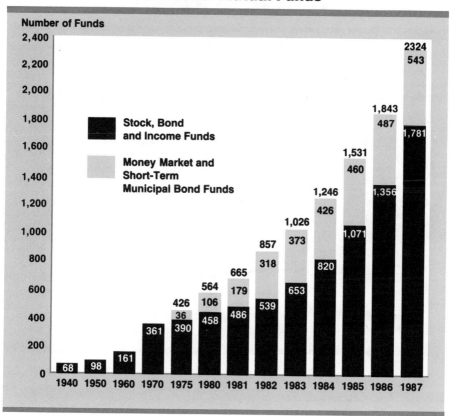

Number of Funds

Legend:
- **Stock, Bond and Income Funds** (dark)
- Money Market and Short-Term Municipal Bond Funds (light)

Year	Stock, Bond and Income	Money Market and Short-Term Municipal Bond	Total
1940	68		
1950	98		
1960	161		
1970	361		
1975	390	36	426
1980	458	106	564
1981	486	179	665
1982	539	318	857
1983	653	373	1,026
1984	820	426	1,246
1985	1,071	460	1,531
1986	1,356	487	1,843
1987	1,781	543	2324

lion in 1980 to $254.7 billion at the end of 1987. Short-term municipal bond fund assets grew from $1.9 billion in 1980 to $61.4 billion. Equity funds had $41.0 billion in 1980 and are now at $180.7 billion in assets. The bond and income fund category has soared from $17.4 billion in 1980 to $273.2 billion at the end of 1987. Combined assets of all funds at the end of 1980 were $134.8 billion. On December 31, 1987, they were $769.9 billion.

The last few years have witnessed a shifting asset mix: from approximately 40 percent long-term and 60 percent short-term in 1983, to roughly 50–50 in 1985, to 60 percent long-term and 40 percent short-term in 1987.

Number of Funds Increases Dramatically

A substantial change has taken place over the years in the number of funds available to investors. In just one decade, the number of funds has increased over 5 times—from 427 funds in 1977 to 2,324 funds at the end of 1987. The increasing variety and number of funds exemplify the enormous change that has occurred in the mutual fund industry.

In the 1950s and 1960s, the industry's historic concentration in equity funds was reflected in an enormous growth in sales and assets of these funds. This growth occurred in a period

Mutual Fund Shareholder Accounts

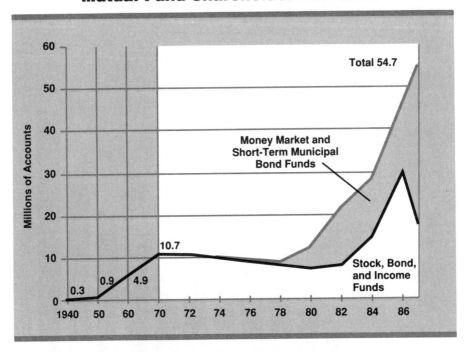

Millions of Accounts

Total 54.7

Money Market and
Short-Term Municipal
Bond Funds

10.7

0.3   0.9   4.9

Stock, Bond,
and Income
Funds

1940   50   60   70   72   74   76   78   80   82   84   86

Assets of Mutual Funds

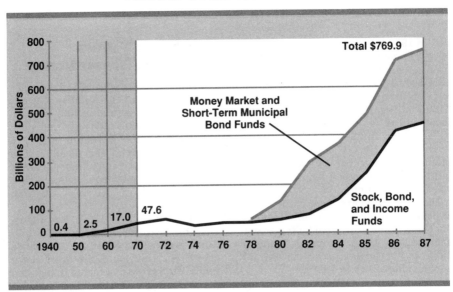

Billions of Dollars

Total $769.9

Money Market and
Short-Term Municipal
Bond Funds

47.6

0.4   2.5   17.0

Stock, Bond,
and Income
Funds

1940   50   60   70   72   74   76   78   80   82   84   85   86   87

14

Sales, Redemptions, and Assets

Equity, Bond, and Income Funds

(Billions of Dollars)

Year	Sales	Redemptions	Net Sales	Assets
1971	$ 5.1	$ 4.8	$ 0.3	$55.0
1972	4.9	6.6	(1.7)	59.8
1973	4.4	5.7	(1.3)	46.5
1974	3.1	3.4	(0.3)	34.1
1975	3.3	3.7	(0.4)	42.2
1976	4.4	6.8	(2.4)	47.6
1977	6.4	6.0	0.4	45.0
1978	6.7	7.2	(0.5)	45.0
1979	6.8	8.0	(1.2)	49.0
1980	10.0	8.2	1.8	58.4
1981	9.7	7.5	2.2	55.2
1982	15.7	7.6	8.1	76.8
1983	40.3	14.7	25.6	113.6
1984	45.9	20.0	25.9	137.1
1985	114.3	33.8	80.5	251.7
1986	215.8	67.0	148.8	424.2
1987	190.6	116.2	74.4	453.8

Money Market Mutual Funds

(Billions of Dollars)

Year	Sales	Redemptions	Net Sales	Assets
1975	$ 6.7	$ 5.9	$ 0.8	$ 3.7
1976	9.4	9.6	(0.2)	3.7
1977	10.7	10.7	0.0	3.9
1978	30.5	24.3	6.2	10.9
1979	111.9	78.4	33.5	45.2
1980	232.2	204.1	28.1	74.4
1981	451.9	346.7	105.2	181.9
1982	581.8	559.6	22.2	206.6
1983	463.0	508.7	(45.7)	162.5
1984	572.0	531.1	40.9	209.7
1985	730.1	732.3	(2.2)	207.5
1986	792.3	776.3	16.0	228.3
1987	869.1	865.7	3.4	254.7

Short-Term Municipal Bond Funds

(Billions of Dollars)

Year	Sales	Redemptions	Net Sales	Assets
1979	$ 0.6	$ 0.4	$ 0.2	$ 0.3
1980	5.3	3.8	1.5	1.9
1981	10.5	8.3	2.2	4.2
1982	29.4	22.2	7.2	13.2
1983	44.5	42.4	2.1	16.8
1984	62.3	55.9	6.4	23.8
1985	109.4	98.8	10.6	36.3
1986	197.5	172.3	25.2	63.8
1987	191.9	196.9	(5.0)	61.4

Net Exchanges by Investment Objective – 1987

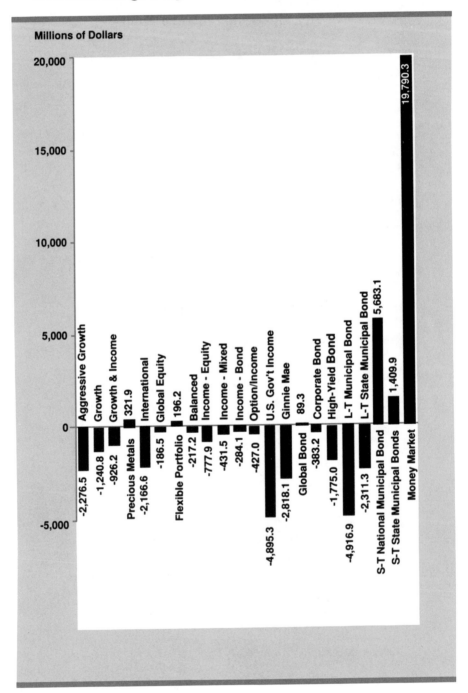

Millions of Dollars

Investment Objective	Value
Aggressive Growth	-2,276.5
Growth	-1,240.8
Growth & Income	-926.2
Precious Metals	321.9
International	-2,166.6
Global Equity	-186.5
Flexible Portfolio	196.2
Balanced	-217.2
Income - Equity	-777.9
Income - Mixed	-431.5
Income - Bond	-284.1
Option/Income	-427.0
U.S. Gov't Income	-4,895.3
Ginnie Mae	-2,818.1
Global Bond	89.3
Corporate Bond	-383.2
High-Yield Bond	-1,775.0
L-T Municipal Bond	-4,916.9
L-T State Municipal Bond	-2,311.3
S-T National Municipal Bond	5,683.1
S-T State Municipal Bonds	1,409.9
Money Market	19,790.3

when stock prices were climbing steadily with only slight interruptions. However, from 1968 to 1974, a weak stock market, rising interest rates, inflation, and other economic and financial uncertainties heightened investor concern about risks associated with equities and dimmed the perception of the funds' potential returns. Consequently, investors stepped away from stocks and equity mutual funds and moved toward the relative safety of short-term liquid assets.

During the mid-1970s, when investor demand for equity products was declining, the industry introduced money market funds, which quickly became very popular with investors. Then came municipal bonds funds, and new versions of standard stock and bond funds, such as international funds, precious metals funds, and, more recently, Ginnie Mae and government income funds. By broadening its product line and encouraging use of the exchange feature within a family of funds, the industry transformed itself into a diversified financial business capable of providing a variety of benefits to both individual and institutional investors.

While the process of reshaping the fund industry was several years in the making, the cumulative impact of the elements within the industry's marketing strategy have come together in recent years. Annual sales of money market funds have more than tripled since 1980, and short-term municipal bond fund sales are more than 36 times their 1980 level. Sales of equity and bond funds have set new record levels during the 1980s, partly due to investor recognition of the excellent performance of both types of funds. Although sales of equity funds did decline at the end of 1987 owing to the sudden stock market drop on October 19, total sales of long-term mutual funds in 1987 set the second highest record ever at $190.6 billion, behind 1986's total of $215.8 billion.

Investors also show an increased awareness of the exchange privilege, which allows mutual fund shareholders to exchange shares from one fund to another within a group of funds under common management. This awareness, along with volatile financial markets, has encouraged investors to be flexible in the handling of their personal portfolios, producing a significant increase in exchange activity.

In 1987, for example, exchanges into all types of mutual funds totaled $205.7 billion, more than 14 times the level in the early part of the decade. As shown in the accompanying chart, total exchanges barely exceeded $14 billion in 1981. Since that date, exchanges have risen at a phenomenal rate. In general, exchange activity over the decade has concentrated in the shifting between long-term equity and bond funds and short-term money market funds as investors adjust their assets to correspond to their changing needs and

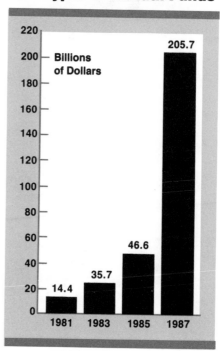

Sales Exchanges
All Types of Mutual Funds

Billions of Dollars

1981: 14.4
1983: 35.7
1985: 46.6
1987: 205.7

to reflect their view of current market conditions. The high level of exchanges in 1987 represents, in part, a response to the October market break as investors exchanged out of equity funds into other types of funds, primarily bond and money market funds.

In a relatively short period of time, mutual funds have become the nation's fourth largest type of financial institution. Only commercial banks, savings and loan institutions, and life insurance companies are larger in terms of assets.

Responding to Investor Needs

One of the hallmarks of the mutual fund industry is its responsiveness in a rapidly changing economic environment.

By keeping attuned to investor needs, the mutual fund industry has been able to adapt and expand its product line and services to suit just about any investor's goals.

As a result, the investor's choice of funds and investment objectives has grown dramatically. In 1975, mutual funds fit neatly into seven main categories. By the end of 1985, the seven fund categories had grown to 15, with many funds further defining their investment objectives according to industry sectors, geographic limitations, or business philosophies. The number of individual funds available almost quadrupled in that period. Continuing innovation in the variety of mutual fund portfolios being offered to the public further increased the investment objective categories in 1987 to 22.

With such a wide range of choices, the often-heard phrase, "Today, there's a mutual fund to meet every investor's needs!" is no exaggeration.

After providing the investing public with funds offering a full range of investment objectives, the industry's next priority has been ensuring prompt, professional service. In addition to the advantages their structure provides (as described on pages 6–9, "What Is a Mutual Fund?"), mutual funds offer a variety of other conveniences.

One such convenience is the ease of entering a fund. Each fund establishes a minimum amount for opening an account plus minimum increments for adding to it. Some funds have very low minimums and others none at all. Still others have minimums of $2,500 and up. The great majority fall between $250 and $1,000.

Funds try to make investing as easy as possible. Most have payroll deduction plans to take the effort out of making regular contributions.

Mutual funds also offer automatic reinvestment programs in which shareholders can elect to have dividends and capital gains distributions poured back into the fund by automatically buying new shares to expand their holdings.

A similar feature covers automatic withdrawal. Arrangements can be made with the fund to send checks automatically from the fund's earnings or principal to the shareholder—or anyone else designated by the shareholder.

Even if a shareholder is not participating in a regular withdrawal plan, the fund makes it easy to withdraw money. By law, the fund must be willing to redeem any or all shares on each business day. All a shareholder needs to do is give proper notification and the fund will send a check. Even easier is a shareholder's ability to write checks drawing from a money market mutual fund account and from some bond funds. While most funds have minimum check amounts of $500, this still proves a convenient way to redeem shares instantly.

If shareholders do not want to withdraw their money but, instead, want to move their assets into a different fund, they can take advantage of a fund's exchange privilege. Many management companies offer more than one fund (known as a "family of funds") to their shareholders. In this way, investors can choose from funds with a vari-

Number of Mutual Funds
Classified by Investment Objective

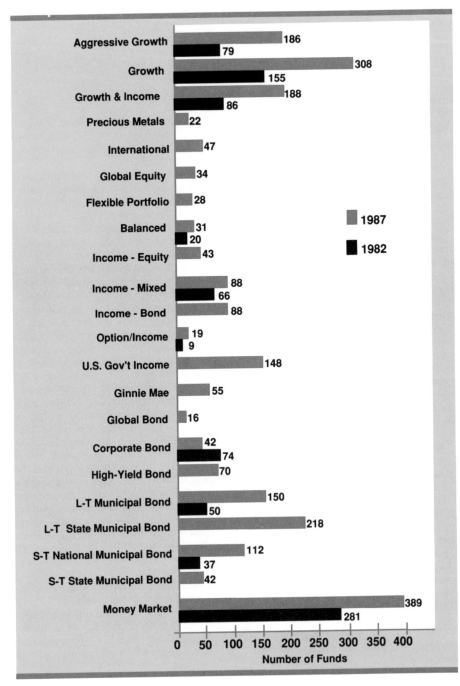

	Number of Funds
Aggressive Growth	186 / 79
Growth	308 / 155
Growth & Income	188 / 86
Precious Metals	22
International	47
Global Equity	34
Flexible Portfolio	28
Balanced	31 / 20
Income - Equity	43
Income - Mixed	88 / 66
Income - Bond	88
Option/Income	19 / 9
U.S. Gov't Income	148
Ginnie Mae	55
Global Bond	16
Corporate Bond	42 / 74
High-Yield Bond	70
L-T Municipal Bond	150 / 50
L-T State Municipal Bond	218
S-T National Municipal Bond	112 / 37
S-T State Municipal Bond	42
Money Market	389 / 281

1987
1982

ety of investment objectives, each appropriate for different investor needs and economic conditions. An exchange privilege allows the shareholder to contact the fund or a fund representative at any time to exchange shares from one fund within the family to another. Usually funds allow investors to use the exchange privilege several times a year for a low or no fee per exchange.

Whenever a shareholder exchanges shares, writes a check from a money market fund, or makes an investment, a statement will be sent to confirm each transaction. Mutual funds have long been noted for their convenient recordkeeping. In addition to confirmation statements, the fund sends account updates on a monthly, quarterly, or annual basis, depending on the fund.

Finally, funds send periodic reports both to the SEC and to shareholders. Complete information is supplied to shareholders at least twice a year, and for most companies, four times a year. These reports list the names and the amount of securities the fund holds. They also show major investment changes since the last report, plus financial statements and related information.

The mutual fund industry tries to stay in tune with the needs of its current *and* future shareholders. Healthy competition ensures that the industry will continue to develop new products and services to respond to the needs of mutual fund shareholders better than ever.

Professional Management

Professional money management is one of the key features that draws investors to mutual funds. It is even more important today when many individuals find it increasingly difficult to make their own way in the securities markets.

The alternatives can seem endless and bewildering. Plus, many people do not have the time, inclination, or experience to choose and manage their own investments. Even individuals who *want* to make their own investment decisions sometimes feel squeezed out of the market by a phenomenon referred to as "the institutionalization of the market." Institutions are playing a much larger role in the securities markets through their big-volume trades executed by large "buy" and "sell" programs that can suddenly affect prices of securities. Takeover activity—and rumored activity—can also cause rapid fluctuations in securities prices. The average investor is finding it tougher and tougher to determine how market activity and fundamental economic changes affect individual securities and industries.

To invest more effectively today, millions of Americans have, in effect, hired professional money managers through mutual fund investing. No matter how modest their holdings, individual investors have joined the institutional investors by choosing mutual funds.

What Do the Money Managers Do?

Fund managers perform extensive economic and financial research. Their aim: to develop data so intelligent decisions can be made about securities in the fund's portfolio.

To make these decisions, investment analysts research basic economic trends—market conditions, interest rates, inflation—and then assess how individual companies and other security-issuing organizations will be affected. Managers read widely . . . not only general business publications, but also trade publications, research reports, and surveys. Their job means keeping up with the steady stream of financial information that companies release and file with various government agencies. They study balance sheets and other financial statements, companies' business systems and marketing philosophies, and talk to a cross-section of business executives. They may make field trips to inspect a com-

Portfolio Composition of Equity, Bond, and Income Funds Yearend 1987
(Billions of Dollars)

Common Stock	$176.4
Preferred Stock	5.6
Municipal Bonds (long-term)	68.6
Corporate Bonds	41.6
U.S. Gov't Sec. (long-term)	119.8
U.S. Gov't Sec. (short-term)	14.2
Liquid Assets	23.8
Other	3.8
Total Net Assets	$453.8

pany's plants. Often they specialize. One analyst may study utilities while a colleague concentrates on the computer industry. A third may study stock markets overseas while another follows bonds or other debt issues.

Those responsible for managing the fund make buy and sell decisions for their portfolio based on this research and the fund's investment objective. Typically, portfolio managers will invest the pool of investment dollars contributed by shareholders in anywhere from 50 to over 100 different securities to diversify the fund's holdings.

Money Market Fund Asset Composition Yearend 1987

(Billions of Dollars)

U.S. Treasury Bills	$4.9
Other Treasury Securities	9.4
Other U.S. Securities	27.0
Repurchase Agreements	39.3
Commercial Bank CDs	24.2
Other Domestic CDs	9.3
Eurodollar CDs	21.6
Commercial Paper	100.6
Bankers Acceptances	10.8
Cash Reserves	(.3)
Other	7.9
Total Net Assets	$254.7
Average Maturity (Days)	31
Number of Funds	389

Diversification

Diversification is a basic investment principle of all mutual funds. It means that the professional managers of mutual funds combine the money of shareholders and invest in many types of securities. It is a proven method of reducing the risk inherent in all investing.

Diversification may take different forms:

• Diversification among a variety of securities issuers—A number of federal and state regulations require this type of diversification. The Investment Company Act of 1940 sets minimum diversification standards for a mutual fund to qualify as a diversified company; the Internal Revenue Code mandates a certain measure of diversification for a fund to qualify as a regulated investment company; and various states impose diversification requirements for a fund to be able to offer its shares in the state.

• Diversification among types of securities—Balanced funds are one example of this form of diversification. These funds invest in common stocks, preferred stocks, and corporate bonds.

• Diversification among a variety of industries—Stock funds diversify their portfolios by including securities issued by companies in many different industries. Corporate bond portfolios also include issues of different types of businesses, while those of municipal bond funds include holdings of a wide range of state and local governments.

• The exceptions—Not all funds are diversified across company, industry, and geographical lines. Specialty funds or sector funds focus on a specific industry, market segment, or geographic region. Examples include funds investing in high technology stocks, the health care industry, or sunbelt companies. But even in specialty funds, money managers still diversify within those specific areas.

Security Selection

In recent years, the huge net sales volume of equity funds has been a major source of liquidity in the securities market and, indirectly, has improved the climate for financing new equity issues. Mutual fund managers must choose from thousands of unknown securities issues with an estimated value of $3.9 trillion available on the organized exchanges and the over-the-counter markets in the U.S.

Mutual Fund Investment Performance
(10 Years through 12/31/87)

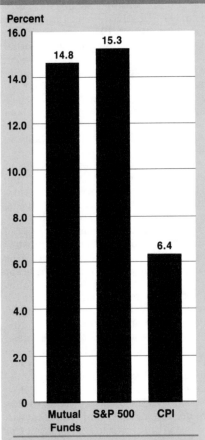

NOTE:
Mutual fund performance reflects a monthly weighted average for all equity funds.

Mutual fund and S&P 500 data prepared by Lipper Analytical Services. These indexes are not adjusted for sales charges.

Money Market Mutual Funds Average Annual Yield

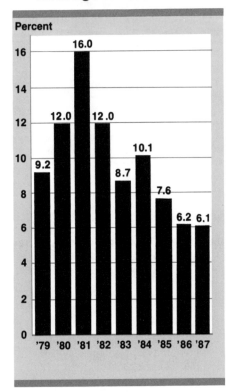

Mutual funds held $182 billion of those stocks in their portfolios in 1987—representing thousands of different securities issues.

Funds purchase substantial amounts of corporate bonds and municipal securities, thereby helping finance corporate America as well as state and local governments. There are approximately $1.9 trillion in corporate and long-term municipal bonds on the market. Mutual funds held $41.6 billion in bonds and $68.6 billion in long-term municipal securities at the end of 1987.

With the strength in sales of government income and Ginnie Mae funds in recent years, the mutual fund industry has become an important market for government-backed mortgage securities, Treasury bonds, and other government securities. They currently hold about $134 billion worth of these securities in their portfolios.

Mutual funds, in short, do the job of an efficient financial intermediary. They gather up the public's savings and channel them into productive uses.

The tables at the end of this chapter represent the dollar value and market percentage for industries of special interest to equity fund managers in 1987. As might be expected, the ranking of various industries and the size of their share in fund portfolios change constantly. These variations reflect portfolio managers' evolving views of the attractiveness of securities from firms in different industry groups.

Dividends and Reinvestment
All Types of Mutual Funds
(Billions of Dollars)

Year	Investment Income Dividends	Reinvested Dividends	Percentage Reinvested
1975	$ 1.6	$ 1.1	68.1%
1976	1.7	1.1	63.1
1977	1.9	1.3	65.8
1978	2.5	1.8	71.3
1979	5.2	3.7	72.2
1980	10.4	8.5	81.3
1981	21.7	19.7	91.7
1982	25.8	22.9	88.8
1983	18.8	15.7	83.5
1984	23.7	18.4	77.6
1985	28.9	20.4	70.6
1986	35.8	25.5	71.2
1987	47.4	30.9	65.2

Capital Gains and Dividends
Distributions to Shareholders
All Types of Mutual Funds
(Billions of Dollars)

Year	Net Realized Capital Gains	Net Investment Income Equity, Bond, and Income Funds	Money Market Funds	Short-Term Municipal Bond Funds
1975	$ 0.2	$ 1.4	$ 0.2	NA
1976	0.5	1.6	0.1	NA
1977	0.6	1.8	0.1	NA
1978	0.7	2.1	0.4	NA
1979	0.9	2.5	2.7	NA
1980	1.7	2.7	7.7	$0.1
1981	2.7	3.1	18.5	0.1
1982	2.4	3.8	21.7	0.3
1983	4.4	5.0	13.2	0.6
1984	6.1	7.3	15.4	1.0
1985	5.0	12.9	14.4	1.6
1986	17.9	22.3	11.1	2.4
1987	23.0	31.8	12.8	2.8

Diversification of Mutual Fund Portfolios
Common Stock Holdings by Industry
(Millions of Dollars)

	1986	1987
Agricultural Equipment	$ 232.4	$ 710.8
Aircraft Manufacturing & Aerospace	1,009.0	1,195.6
Air Transport	1,093.5	1,720.4
Auto & Accessories (excl. Tires)	2,792.1	3,853.7
Building Materials & Equipment	1,175.8	1,537.9
Chemicals	3,310.4	4,394.7
Communications (TV, Radio, Motion Pictures, Telephone)	3,979.3	5,618.2
Computer Services*	512.8	880.6
Conglomerates	1,370.0	2,003.0
Containers	305.5	632.2
Drugs & Cosmetics	4,025.3	4,587.7
Electric Equipment & Electronics (excl. TV & Radio)	4,499.9	8,047.0
Financial (incl. Banks & Insurance)	11,046.2	13,049.2
Foods and Beverages	1,843.8	2,146.6
Hospital Supplies & Services	867.0	1,107.4
Leisure Time	1,699.9	1,702.9
Machinery	767.4	1,487.1
Metals & Mining	1,819.6	3,221.9
Office Equipment	3,016.5	3,709.9
Oil	2,988.4	5,474.4
Paper	2,168.1	1,869.2
Printing & Publishing	907.9	1,295.0
Public Utilities (incl. Natural Gas)	4,347.6	5,097.3
Railroads & Railroad Equipment	570.4	1,435.6
Retail Trade	3,939.7	4,757.3
Rubber (incl. Tires)	458.1	628.0
Steel	184.8	443.4
Textiles	417.5	456.2
Tobacco	911.7	933.2
Miscellaneous	2,198.4	3,092.2
Total	**$64,459.0**	**$87,088.6**

Note: Composite industry investments drawn from the portfolios of 60 of the largest investment companies as of the end of the calendar year 1987 whose total net assets represented 51.8% of total net assets of all reporting equity companies. Previous years not shown due to change in sample.

*Includes computer software, consultants and time sharing.

Diversification of Mutual Fund Portfolios
Percent of Total Common Stock by Industry

	1986	1987
Agricultural Equipment	0.36%	0.82%
Aircraft Manufacturing & Aerospace	1.57	1.37
Air Transport	1.70	1.98
Auto & Accessories (excl. Tires)	4.33	4.42
Building Materials & Equipment	1.82	1.77
Chemicals	5.14	5.04
Communications (TV, Radio, Motion Pictures, Telephone)	6.17	6.45
Computer Services*	0.80	1.01
Conglomerates	2.13	2.30
Containers	0.47	0.73
Drugs & Cosmetics	6.24	5.27
Electric Equipment & Electronics (excl. TV & Radio)	6.98	9.24
Financial (incl. Banks & Insurance)	17.14	14.98
Foods and Beverages	2.86	2.46
Hospital Supplies & Services	1.35	1.27
Leisure Time	2.64	1.96
Machinery	1.19	1.71
Metals & Mining	2.82	3.70
Office Equipment	4.68	4.26
Oil	4.64	6.29
Paper	3.36	2.15
Printing & Publishing	1.41	1.49
Public Utilities (incl. Natural Gas)	6.74	5.85
Railroads & Railroad Equipment	0.88	1.65
Retail Trade	6.11	5.46
Rubber (incl. Tires)	0.71	0.72
Steel	0.29	0.51
Textiles	0.65	0.52
Tobacco	1.41	1.07
Miscellaneous	3.41	3.55
Total	**100.00**	**100.00**

Note: Composite industry investments drawn from the portfolios of 60 of the largest investment companies as of the end of the calendar year 1987 whose total net assets represented 51.8% of total net assets of all reporting equity companies. Previous years not shown due to change in sample.

*Includes computer software, consultants and time sharing.

Recent Trends in Activity:
Stock, Bond, and Income Funds

ales of stock, bond, and income funds in 1987 totaled $190.6 billion, the second highest total ever. While this amount is less than the recordsetting 1986 total of $215.8 billion, the 1987 figure is $76.3 billion more than the total amount of sales of stock, bond, and income funds in 1985, and more than four times total sales in 1984.

Owing to a strong first three quarters' performance, total stock fund sales were higher in 1987 than in 1986, $72.1 billion compared to $57.7 billion, respectively. However, the sales total for bond and income funds of $118.6 billion in 1987 was down from the 1986 total of $158.1 billion.

The leading stock fund category in 1987 was growth and income funds with $23.3 billion in sales, followed by growth funds with $17.7 billion, and aggressive growth funds with $11.7 billion. Sales of precious metals funds

Share of Equity Funds
Sales and Redemptions Annually

	Sales		Redemptions	
	1986	1987	1986	1987
Aggressive Growth	17.2%	16.3%	19.5%	17.9%
Growth	21.6	24.6	29.5	27.2
Growth & Income	32.6	32.4	28.4	27.3
Precious Metals	1.1	4.4	2.5	4.6
International	7.2	5.8	6.4	7.6
Global-Equity	5.4	4.3	4.5	5.0
Income Equity	9.5	9.4	5.1	6.8
Option/Income	5.4	2.8	4.1	3.6
Total	100.0%	100.0%	100.0%	100.0%

Share of Bond and Income Funds
Sales and Redemptions Annually

	Sales		Redemptions	
	1986	1987	1986	1987
Flexible Portfolio	0.3%	2.5%	0.4%	0.7%
Balanced	2.1	2.8	1.3	1.5
Income-Mixed	4.3	5.0	8.5	6.3
Income-Bond	3.4	4.5	4.1	4.2
U.S. Government Income	34.4	37.1	35.3	36.0
Ginnie Mae	18.3	11.2	17.5	17.1
Global Bond	0.3	0.9	0.1	0.6
Corporate Bond	2.8	3.1	2.2	2.9
High-Yield Bond	8.9	8.5	7.9	7.8
Long-Term Municipal Bond	15.6	15.2	16.0	15.4
Long-Term State Municipal Bond	9.6	9.2	6.7	7.5
Total	100.0%	100.0%	100.0%	100.0%

Mutual Fund Assets
Classified by Investment Objective

(Billions of Dollars)

Yearend

Investment Objective	1986	1987	Percent Change
Aggressive Growth	$ 25.0	$ 27.3	+ 9.2%
Growth	43.6	48.0	+ 10.1
Growth & Income	55.9	64.0	+ 14.5
Precious Metals	2.0	4.1	+105.0
International	7.2	7.0	− 2.8
Global Equity	8.3	10.4	+ 25.3
Flexible Portfolio	1.5	4.3	+186.7
Balanced	7.5	9.0	+ 20.0
Income-Equity	12.6	14.7	+ 16.7
Income-Mixed	10.3	11.4	+ 10.7
Income-Bond	11.4	12.6	+ 10.5
Option/Income	7.0	5.1	− 27.1
U.S. Government Income	82.4	88.9	+ 7.9
Ginnie Mae	39.6	34.2	− 13.6
Global Bond	0.5	2.1	+320.0
Corporate Bond	9.1	9.5	+ 4.4
High-Yield Bond	24.6	24.2	− 1.6
Long-Term Municipal Bond	49.9	49.2	− 1.4
Long-Term State Municipal Bond	25.8	27.8	+ 7.8
*Total Long-Term Funds	$424.2	$453.8	+ 7.0%

Mutual Fund Sales
Classified by Investment Objective

(Millions of Dollars)

Investment Objective	1986	1987	Percent Change
Aggressive Growth	$ 9,928.2	$ 11,732.5	+ 18.2%
Growth	12,459.3	17,723.5	+ 42.3
Growth & Income	18,811.0	23,320.1	+ 24.0
Precious Metals	656.6	3,180.8	+384.4
International	4,169.8	4,183.6	+ 0.3
Global Equity	3,118.0	3,130.4	+ 0.4
Flexible Portfolio	520.6	2,966.3	+469.8
Balanced	3,341.0	3,263.4	− 2.3
Income-Equity	5,470.3	6,760.2	+ 23.6
Income-Mixed	6,799.9	5,915.5	− 13.0
Income-Bond	5,435.5	5,400.6	− 0.6
Option/Income	3,103.5	2,011.1	− 35.2
U.S. Government Income	54,446.3	44,033.0	− 19.1
Ginnie Mae	28,860.2	13,251.1	− 54.1
Global Bond	439.2	1,118.7	+154.7
Corporate Bond	4,430.1	3,683.5	− 16.9
High-Yield Bond	13,978.9	10,020.1	− 28.3
Long-Term Municipal Bond	24,660.0	17,991.1	− 27.0
Long-Term State Municipal Bond	15,219.4	10,918.9	− 28.2
*Total Long-Term Funds	$215,847.8	$190,604.4	− 11.7%

*See next chapter for total short-term fund (money,market and short-term municipal bond funds) assets.

29

reached $3.2 billion, which represented a substantial increase over 1986 sales of $0.7 billion.

In spite of record stock fund sales and a decline in bond and income fund sales, this latter fund type continued the trend of recent years and outsold stock funds by a wide margin. The 1987 figure of $118.6 billion in bond and income fund sales is substantially higher than the $72.1 billion of equity fund sales in 1987. In the bond and income category, global bond funds exhibited the largest percentage increase: a 155 percent jump in sales in 1987 to more than $1 billion from $0.4 billion in 1986.

Since 1987 was a notably volatile year, it is not surprising that the type of fund with the most dramatic leap in sales was flexible portfolio funds, which allow their portfolio managers wide latitude in shifting from all equity securities to all bond securities or money market securities, or any combination thereof, as market condi-

Sales and Redemptions Equity Funds
Annually 1972-1987
(Billions of Dollars)

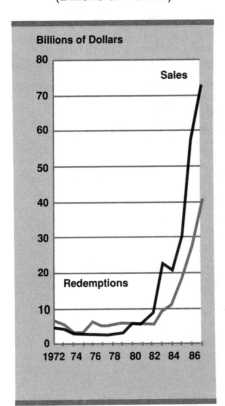

Sales and Redemptions Bond and Income Funds
Annually 1972-1987
(Billions of Dollars)

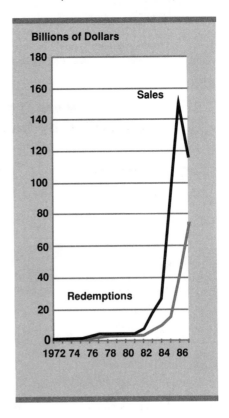

Assets of Equity, Bond, and Income Funds
(Billions of Dollars)

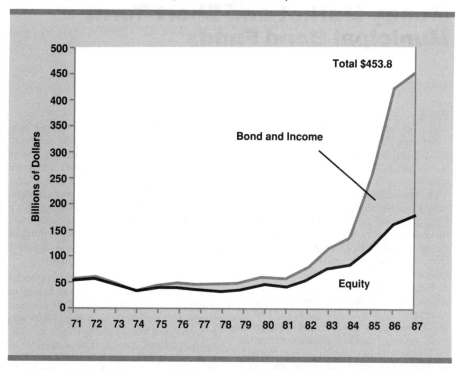

tions warrant. In 1986, flexible portfolio fund sales barely exceeded $0.5 billion, but in 1987 sales reached nearly $3 billion, a whopping 470 percent increase. One reason for these notable increases, in addition to the attractiveness of the investments, is that they are newly identified categories that have only been offered in the last few years.

Four years ago, falling interest rates propelled many investors into newer, more income-oriented funds such as government and Ginnie Mae funds. Here, they obtained attractive real rates of return by assuming moderate levels of risk relative to some other investment options. Many of these investors may have been attracted to mutual funds several years earlier through money market funds. But as the economic climate changed, these same investors turned to other types of funds. Today, investors enjoy a wide

choice of funds such as government funds, Ginnie Mae funds, municipal bond funds, corporate bond funds, income funds, and option/income funds. While these funds all experienced gains in sales in 1986, sales for each type decreased in 1987. Nevertheless, total industry assets in 1987 for these types of funds reached a record high of $453.8 billion, compared with $424.2 billion at the end of 1986, and $251.7 billion at the end of 1985. Assets at the beginning of the decade were only $49 billion.

Increased assets in each broad type of fund resulted in the industry total closing the year at new heights, with assets reaching $769.9 billion by yearend 1987. In comparison, assets at the end of 1986 were $716.2 billion, and $495.5 billion at the end of 1985. Assets at the beginning of the decade were only $94.5 billion.

Recent Trends in Activity:
Money Market and Short-Term Municipal Bond Funds

Total assets of money market funds (MMFs) ended the year at $254.7 billion, an 11 percent increase from the 1986 yearend total of $228.3 billion.

This total marks an all-time high in assets, exceeding the previous record of $232.1 billion in 1982. Money market fund assets have been steadily increasing over the past four years, a far cry from the roller coaster these assets had taken previously. From the 1982 figure of $232.1 billion, money market fund assets plummeted over $60 billion a year later to $162.5 billion at the end of 1983 owing to the competition from both money market deposit accounts (MMDAs) that banks were newly authorized to offer, and rising stock and bond prices. But then the situation leveled off. Since August 1983, MMF rates have consistently been higher than those of the MMDAs, and 1984 saw the industry recoup much of its losses, ending that year at $209.7 billion.

Despite the fact that 1987 was marked by relatively low levels in short-term interest rates, and therefore low rates in the money market, the money market fund assets still managed to post an increase. The same money market fund investors who a few years earlier had been accustomed to yields of 9, 10, and 12 percent (see chart, p. 24), realized yields of about 6 percent for 1987.

In part, the increase in money market fund assets resulted from exchanges out of equity funds after the events of October 1987. But the attractiveness of money market funds also lies in their versatility.

There are three main ways people use money market funds. These vary in importance, depending on market conditions. One major way to use a money market fund is as a cash management tool—a way to earn market rates on money to be used for paying the common bills of everyday life. (Institutions use money market funds this way on a larger scale.) Another is as a savings instrument. And third, money market funds are used as a safe harbor between financial transactions.

Investors have come to recognize the importance of money market funds in every financial plan. For that reason, there will probably be a relatively stable, ongoing use of these funds as cash management tools. The amount of money people keep in these funds may fluctuate with the changing forces in the market, but money market funds will continue to play a role in responding to investors' needs for a relatively safe, high-yielding, liquid instrument.

There are three broad types of money market funds offering shares—each responding to somewhat different needs. General purpose funds and broker/dealer funds, for example, both sell to individuals and to institutions. Individuals, however, are the primary market and represent almost 75 percent of the assets of both types of funds. Conversely, institutional funds concentrate primarily on institutional investors such as businesses and bank trust departments. These funds are characterized by fewer shareholders with larger amounts to invest.

At the end of 1987, of the $254.7 billion in assets, $106.7 billion or 42 percent was in the broker/dealer funds. General purpose funds had $78.3 billion and institutional funds held $69.7

Weekly Yield on MMFs and MMDAs
January 1, 1986 - December 31,1987

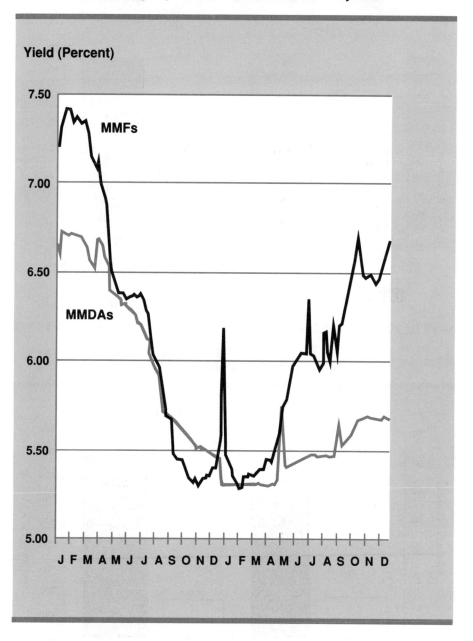

Money Market Fund Assets and Shareholder Accounts

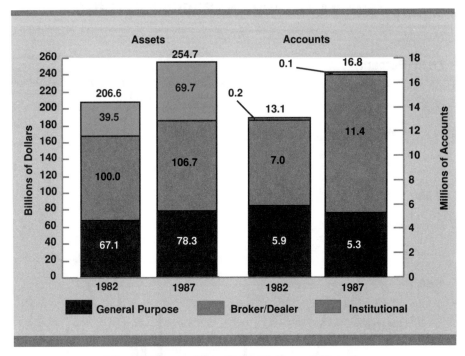

Assets   Accounts

Billions of Dollars — Millions of Accounts

	1982	1987	1982	1987
Total	206.6	254.7	0.2 / 13.1	0.1 / 16.8
Broker/Dealer	39.5	69.7		11.4
Institutional	100.0	106.7	7.0	
General Purpose	67.1	78.3	5.9	5.3

General Purpose   Broker/Dealer   Institutional

Short-Term Municipal Bond Funds
Assets and Shareholder Accounts

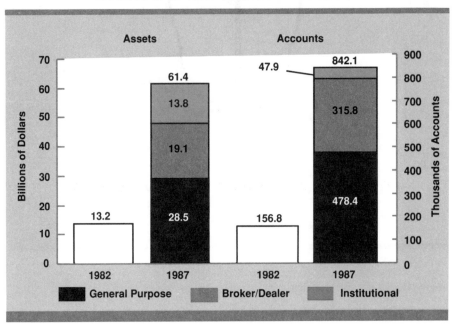

Assets   Accounts

Billions of Dollars — Thousands of Accounts

	1982	1987	1982	1987
Total	13.2	61.4	156.8	47.9 / 842.1
Broker/Dealer		13.8		315.8
Institutional		19.1		
General Purpose		28.5		478.4

General Purpose   Broker/Dealer   Institutional

billion, 31 percent and 27 percent respectively.

Shareholder accounts in money market funds have risen in 1987 to a new record level of 16.8 million. Again, the broker/dealer funds held the largest portion of accounts, making up 68 percent of the market, while general purpose funds accounted for 31 percent. As noted earlier, institutional funds have fewer accounts with large account balances. These funds represent less than 1 percent of all money market fund accounts.

While the money market funds were growing at a healthy rate in 1987, their tax-exempt counterparts, short-term municipal bond funds, were experiencing less investment activity than had occurred in the previous year. These funds, introduced in 1979 with assets of $0.3 billion, ended 1987 with $61.4 billion in assets. In 1986 they had assets of $63.8 billion. Since part of the appeal of these funds (sometimes referred to as tax-exempt money market funds) is the combination of standard money market fund features with the bonus of tax-free income, the lower tax rates imposed by the Tax Reform Act of 1986 undoubtedly accounted for some of the diminished investor interest.

The continued growth in accounts of short-term municipal bond funds demonstrates the appeal they have for investors. Total accounts rose in 1987 to 842,124, compared with 659,600 accounts in 1986, indicating that they are a significant product in the diverse mutual fund marketplace.

How Mutual Fund Shares Are Acquired by Investors

Many kinds of firms provide a wide range of products and services in today's securities industry. Some offer investment advice, financial planning, insurance and commodity products, in addition to such traditional services as executing orders to buy and sell securities and underwriting new stock and bond issues. Some firms offer a few of these products and services, while others only execute trades for investors who have made their own investment decisions.

Considering the securities industry's complexity, it is not surprising that mutual funds' distribution patterns have become equally diverse. Some funds offer their shares to investors through the mail, by telephone, or at their own offices while others sell through securities firms, financial planners, life insurance organizations, other financial institutions, or even through membership organizations.

Basically, however, mutual fund distribution can be broken down into two major channels: shares purchased from a member of a sales force and shares purchased directly from a fund. (In the data section, these two channels are referred to as Sales Force and Direct Marketing.)

Most mutual funds are affiliated with an underwriter that distributes their shares nationally. The underwriter has exclusive distribution rights and may use several different avenues for share distribution.

The Broker/Dealer: Most often, the underwriter distributes fund shares through securities firms and their brokers. These brokers deal directly with the public—the potential purchasers of mutual fund shares.

In addition to traditional broker/dealer firms, an increasing number of financial planners are recommending mutual funds to their clients. More and more, financial planners suggest mutual funds as building blocks in a master financial plan, which might also include life insurance and individual securities.

Within the broker/dealer distribution system, underwriters, in effect, act as wholesalers. Underwriters do not sell shares to the public directly. Instead, they establish sales agreements with securities firms who, in turn, sell the fund's shares to individual investors through the firms' branch offices. To assist local firms and branches, a mutual fund underwriter usually divides the country into regions and assigns its own staff members to represent the underwriter in each area.

Retail securities firms distributing mutual fund shares are usually members of the National Association of Securities Dealers, Inc. This organization provides self-policing of its member firms in the distribution of mutual fund shares, as well as in over-the-counter securities transactions.

Dedicated Sales Force: In some cases, an underwriter employs its own sales force. These people primarily sell shares of the funds the underwriter represents plus other securities issued by the underwriter and its affiliates. In some cases, a dedicated sales force is the sales arm of an insurance company which might own a mutual fund management company.

Sales of Sales Force & Direct Marketing Funds by Investment Objective - 1987 (Percent)

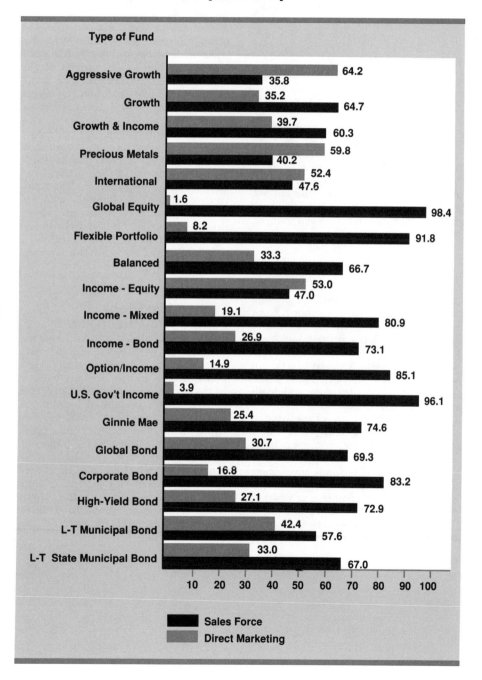

Type of Fund

Type of Fund	Sales Force	Direct Marketing
Aggressive Growth	64.2	35.8
Growth	64.7	35.2
Growth & Income	60.3	39.7
Precious Metals	40.2	59.8
International	47.6	52.4
Global Equity	98.4	1.6
Flexible Portfolio	91.8	8.2
Balanced	66.7	33.3
Income - Equity	47.0	53.0
Income - Mixed	80.9	19.1
Income - Bond	73.1	26.9
Option/Income	85.1	14.9
U.S. Gov't Income	96.1	3.9
Ginnie Mae	74.6	25.4
Global Bond	69.3	30.7
Corporate Bond	83.2	16.8
High-Yield Bond	72.9	27.1
L-T Municipal Bond	57.6	42.4
L-T State Municipal Bond	67.0	33.0

■ Sales Force
▨ Direct Marketing

Fund shares sold through brokers, commission-based financial planners, or dedicated sales forces may have a sales charge included in their offering price. Depending on the type of fund, the charge (usually referred to as a "load") may range from 4 to 8.5 percent. Usually, the basic charge will vary, depending on the size of the purchase. In addition, some funds assign a small percentage of fund assets to aid in distribution expenses. In some cases, there is no up-front sales charge or load, but there may be a charge if shares are redeemed during the first few years of ownership. There may also be an annual fee of one percent or so.

Mutual funds are required to redeem outstanding shares at their current net asset value each day. This is the case regardless of distribution method or commission structure.

Fund to Investor: In this method of distribution, investors purchase mutual fund shares directly from the fund—usually by mail, telephone, bank wire, or sometimes at offices maintained by fund organizations. As a technical matter, however, these direct marketing funds usually have an underwriter—a distribution arm of the fund organization—through which all share transactions pass.

The funds attract investors through advertising, direct mail, and other means. Potential investors do their own research and take the initiative to determine if specific funds meet their needs. Investors contact the fund organization directly to obtain a prospectus or buy shares. The shares of these funds are generally sold to the public with a low sales charge or none at all.

Sales by Method of Distribution

Of all stock, bond, and income fund sales made in the mutual fund industry in 1987, $132.0 billion or 69 percent were made by those funds distributed through a sales force. Those funds distributed directly to investors had sales of $53.1 billion or 28 percent of the total. (Other sales result from reinvested dividends in funds no longer offering shares and from variable annuities.)

Among equity funds, the two major methods of distribution—through a sales force or direct marketing—recorded sales of $38.7 billion and $29.5 billion, respectively. The sales force distribution channels attained their highest percentage of overall sales through $93.3 billion in bond and income fund sales. Direct marketing sales were $23.6 billion in the bond and income funds.

Where the Most Funds Are Purchased

Assets and sales of mutual funds are heaviest in geographic regions with large numbers of people in moderate- to upper-income groups. As may be seen in the accompanying chart, California and New York accounted for the two largest state shares of total sales of equity, bond, and income funds. Sales in California totaled $21.6 billion in 1987, 11.7 percent of all sales of those funds. New York fund sales accounted for $18.7 billion, 10.1 percent of total sales. The ten states with the largest share of stock and bond fund sales, moreover, accounted for over 60 percent of the total.

Equity, Bond, and Income Fund Sales
by Selected States—1987

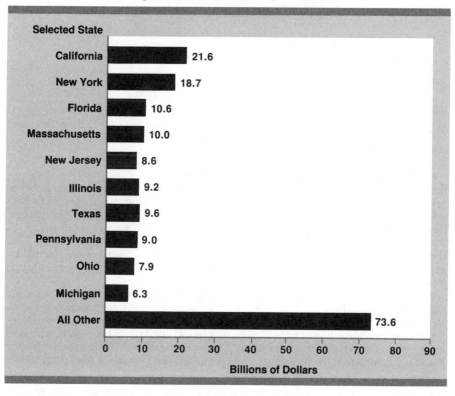

Selected State

State	Billions of Dollars
California	21.6
New York	18.7
Florida	10.6
Massachusetts	10.0
New Jersey	8.6
Illinois	9.2
Texas	9.6
Pennsylvania	9.0
Ohio	7.9
Michigan	6.3
All Other	73.6

Billions of Dollars

The Retirement Market

Mutual funds are especially compatible with the long-term objectives of saving for retirement because:

• There is a fund to match any long-term objective and risk/reward preference.

• Families of funds provide great flexibility through the exchange feature, enabling shareholders to adjust their holdings to economic conditions as well as to changes in their personal financial circumstances.

• Mutual funds work best over long periods of time, when allowed to ride out the ups and downs of market cycles.

• Funds provide a wide range of services, such as automatic withdrawal plans and complete recordkeeping.

(See box on page 44 for descriptions of various retirement plans.)

IRAs

The Individual Retirement Account (IRA) market has rapidly grown to command the largest share of the mutual fund industry's retirement assets.

Although the Tax Reform Act of 1986 modified the ground rules for IRAs, they are still a strong mutual fund market.

In 1981, before IRAs were liberalized to allow all working Americans to create do-it-yourself retirement programs, mutual funds had only $2.6 billion of assets in 500,000 IRA accounts. By the end of 1987, mutual fund IRA assets

IRA Assets by Type of Fund

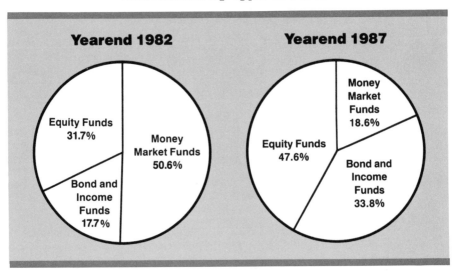

Yearend 1982

Equity Funds 31.7%

Money Market Funds 50.6%

Bond and Income Funds 17.7%

Yearend 1987

Money Market Funds 18.6%

Equity Funds 47.6%

Bond and Income Funds 33.8%

had climbed to $72.2 billion in 15 million accounts. Compared to 1986, mutual fund IRA assets increased by $18.5 billion, and the number of accounts increased by 3.3 million. Of the industry's $72.2 billion in IRA assets, $34.3 billion or 47.5 percent of assets were in equity funds, $24.5 billion or 33.9 percent of assets were in bond and income funds, and $13.4 billion or 18.6 percent were in money market funds.

Of the 15 million IRA accounts, 7.9 million are in equity funds, 3.4 million are in bond and income funds, and 3.7 are in money market funds.

At the end of 1981, when IRAs were liberalized, only 1 percent of all mutual fund assets were held in IRA accounts. At the end of 1987, that share had grown to 9 percent.

In addition, 27 percent of all mutual fund accounts are IRA accounts. (Some IRA mutual fund shareholders hold multiple accounts.)

At the end of 1981, when all Americans with earned income became eligible for IRAs, mutual funds accounted for 9.9 percent of all IRA assets in the marketplace. Growth in mutual fund IRA assets since that time has occurred at a greater rate than growth in competing investments, resulting in an increased share of the IRA market for mutual funds. Mutual funds in 1987 accounted for about 22 percent of the total IRA market.

The Tax Reform Act of 1986 brought significant changes to IRAs (see the boxed section in this chapter on page 44). Nevertheless, about 87 percent of American households are still able to take full or partial IRA deduction. For instance, any individual who is not covered by an employer-provided pension plan, and whose spouse is not covered by an employer-provided pension plan, can take the full IRA deduction without regard to the amount of earned income. Furthermore, the tax deferral that IRAs provide is a powerful wealth-building tool. Other positive factors that will affect the mutual fund IRA market in the future include the large number of outstanding IRA accounts held elsewhere whose owners may turn to mutual funds for improved performance, the benefit of professional money management, and the convenience of recordkeeping that funds offer IRA shareholders. Thus, IRAs should continue to be an important market for mutual funds in the post tax-reform environment.

Estimated Value of IRA Plans
(Value in Billions of Dollars/Percent Market Share)

	12/83		12/85		12/87	
Commercial Banks	$26.5	29.0%	$51.5	25.8%	$77.0	23.1%
Thrifts	31.7	34.7	56.4	28.2	77.1	23.1
Life Insurance Companies	9.0	9.9	16.9	8.5	26.0	7.8
Credit Unions	5.0	5.5	13.9	7.0	22.6	6.8
Mutual Funds	10.7	11.7	31.6	15.8	72.2	21.6
Self Directed	8.4	9.2	29.4	14.7	58.9	17.6
Total IRA Dollar Value	**$91.3**		**$199.7**		**$333.8**	

Retirement Plans for the Self-Employed

Mutual funds, traditionally holding close to a third of the market for retirement plans for the self-employed (also known as Keogh plans), had more than 850,000 of these accounts under management at the end of 1987. These plans totaled $10.1 billion in assets.

As may be seen in the accompanying chart, 48.9 percent of these retirement plans' assets managed by mutual funds were in equity funds, 30.5 percent were in money market funds, and 20.6 percent were in bond and income funds.

The self-employed retirement plan market has become increasingly important since the liberalization of the tax laws in 1982. This change eliminated most of the distinctions between corporate plans and plans maintained for the self-employed, and allowed self-employed individuals to put away the lesser of 25 percent of income or $30,000.

Although the law no longer distinguishes between plans for the self-employed and corporate pension plans, many new restrictions apply to any plan which is a "top-heavy" plan, i.e., a plan under which a substantial portion of the benefits accrue on behalf of cer-

tain key employees of the employer. Many Keogh plans are treated as "top-heavy" plans subject to the aforementioned restrictions. Many mutual fund complexes offer prototype "top-heavy" plans which comply with all of the new provisions of law.

Self-Employed Retirement Plan Assets by Type of Fund Yearend 1987

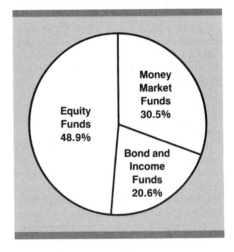

Equity Funds 48.9%

Money Market Funds 30.5%

Bond and Income Funds 20.6%

Mutual Fund IRAs by Investment Objective

Investment Objective	Percent of Assets as of 12/31/87
Aggressive Growth	10.4%
Growth	10.6
Growth & Income	15.0
Precious Metals	1.1
International	1.5
Global Equity	3.0
Flexible Portfolio	0.3
Balanced	1.4
Income-Equity	4.9
Income-Mixed	1.6
Income-Bond	2.3
Option/Income	1.1
U.S. Government Income	14.2
Ginnie Mae	5.8
Global Bond	0.2
Corporate Bond	2.1
High-Yield Bond	5.9
Money Market	18.6

Growth in Mutual Funds IRA Plans 1987

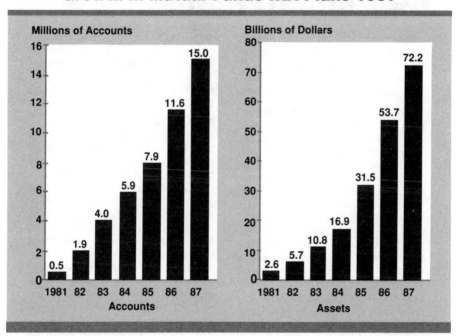

Millions of Accounts

Year	Accounts
1981	0.5
82	1.9
83	4.0
84	5.9
85	7.9
86	11.6
87	15.0

Accounts

Billions of Dollars

Year	Assets
1981	2.6
82	5.7
83	10.8
84	16.9
85	31.5
86	53.7
87	72.2

Assets

Growth in Mutual Funds Self-Employed Retirement Plans 1987

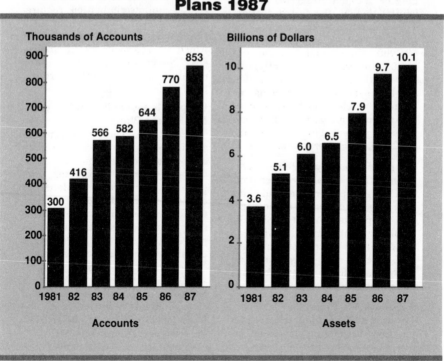

Thousands of Accounts

Year	Accounts
1981	300
82	416
83	566
84	582
85	644
86	770
87	853

Accounts

Billions of Dollars

Year	Assets
1981	3.6
82	5.1
83	6.0
84	6.5
85	7.9
86	9.7
87	10.1

Assets

Retirement Plans

Federal income tax laws permit the establishment of a number of types of retirement plans, each of which may be funded with mutual fund shares.

Individual Retirement Accounts

All wage earners under the age of 70½ may set up an Individual Retirement Account (IRA). The individual may contribute as much as 100 percent of his or her compensation each year, up to $2,000. Earnings are tax-deferred until withdrawal. The amount contributed each year may be wholly or partially tax-deductible. Under the Tax Reform Act of 1986, all taxpayers not covered by employer-sponsored retirement plans can continue to take the full deduction for IRA contributions. Those who are covered or who are married to someone who is covered must have an adjusted gross income of no more than $25,000 (single) or $40,000 (married, filing jointly) to take the full deduction. The deduction is phased out for incomes between $25,000 and $35,000 (single) and $40,000 and $50,000 (married, filing jointly). An individual who qualifies for an IRA and has a spouse who either has no earnings or elects to be treated as having no earnings, may contribute up to 100 percent of his or her income or $2,250, whichever is less.

Simplified Employee Pensions

Simplified Employee Pensions (SEPs) are employer-sponsored plans that may be viewed as an aggregation of separate IRAs. In an SEP, the employer contribution, limited to $30,000 or 15 percent of compensation, whichever is less, is made to an Individual Retirement Account maintained for the employee.

Section 403(b) Plans

Section 403(b) of the Internal Revenue Code permits employees of certain charitable organizations and public school systems to establish tax-sheltered retirement programs. These plans may be invested in either annuity contracts or mutual fund shares.

Section 401(k) Plans

One particularly popular type of plan which may be offered by either corporate or noncorporate entities is the 401(k) plan. A 401(k) plan is a tax-qualified profit-sharing plan that includes a "cash or deferred" arrangement. The cash or deferred arrangement permits employees to have a portion of their compensation contributed to a tax-sheltered plan on their behalf or paid to them directly as additional taxable compensation. Thus an employee may elect to reduce his or her taxable compensation with contributions to a 401(k) plan where those amounts will accumulate tax-free. The Tax Reform Act of 1986 established new, tighter antidiscrimination requirements for 401(k) plans and curtailed the amount of elective deferrals which may be made by all employees. Nevertheless, 401(k) plans remain excellent and popular retirement savings vehicles.

Corporate and Self-Employed Retirement Plans

Tax-qualified pension and profit-sharing plans may be established by corporations or self-employed individuals. Changes in the tax laws have made retirement plans for employees of corporations and those for self-employed individuals essentially comparable. Contributions to a plan are tax-deductible and earnings accumulate on a tax-sheltered basis.

The maximum annual amount which may be contributed to a defined contribution plan on behalf of an individual is limited to the lesser of 25 percent of the individual's compensation or $30,000.

Corporate Plans

In recent years, mutual funds have made substantial progress in attracting corporate pension and profit-sharing accounts. Corporate plan sponsors have come to appreciate the built-in advantages mutual funds can offer their plans. Mutual funds give them access to top professional money managers, instant diversification, a portfolio managed according to a well-defined philosophy and policy, liquidity, and ease of administration.

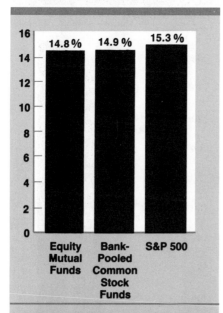

Comparative Equity Performance Annualized 10-Year Total Return
(Period Ending December 31, 1987)

Source: ICI monthly asset weighted average equity fund performance and the S&P 500 returns were compiled by Lipper Analytical Services. The bank-pooled common stock fund asset weighted returns from data are compiled by CDA, Inc.

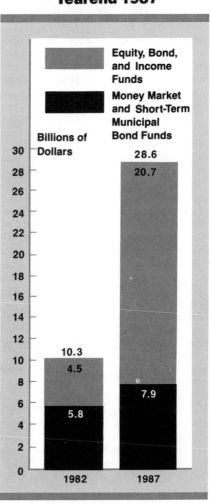

Total Net Assets Held in Pension and Profit Sharing Accounts in Mutual Funds Yearend 1987

Institutional Markets

Perhaps more than most other investments, mutual funds are especially important to small investors. The modest initial investment requirements, plus investors' ability to add relatively small amounts to their accounts at regular intervals help explain why mutual funds are so popular to this group. Outstanding investment performance, diversification, and other services available through mutual funds, however, also attract fund investors in middle- and upper-income brackets. But these groups are not alone in their enthusiastic embrace of mutual funds. Increasingly, institutions are turning to mutual funds as an investment option.

Banks and other fiduciaries, business corporations, employee pension and profit-sharing plans, insurance companies, and foundations are among the institutions utilizing mutual funds. As the accompanying chart shows, the value of institutional assets under management has risen from about $6.2 billion in 1970 to $271.3 billion at the end of 1987.

Since this rate of growth has been much more rapid than the expansion of assets owned by individuals, institutional assets have accounted for an expanding share of total mutual fund assets. Between the end of 1960 and the end of 1987, the share of total assets accounted for by institutions rose from 10.6 percent to 35.2 percent. Part of the reason for the acceleration in institutional activity has been the expansion of money market funds, which were first offered in the mid-1970s.

Institutional assets represented 48.5 percent of total money market fund

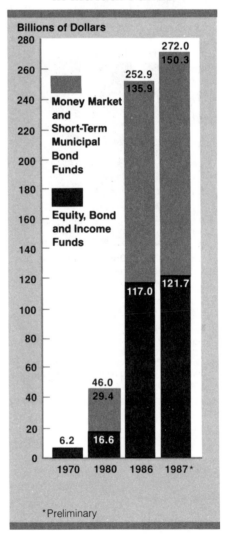

Total Institutional Assets in Mutual Funds

Billions of Dollars

Money Market and Short-Term Municipal Bond Funds

Equity, Bond and Income Funds

	1970	1980	1986	1987*
Total	6.2	46.0	252.9	272.0
Money Market		29.4	135.9	150.3
Equity/Bond		16.6	117.0	121.7

*Preliminary

Institutional Assets by Type of Institution—1987*

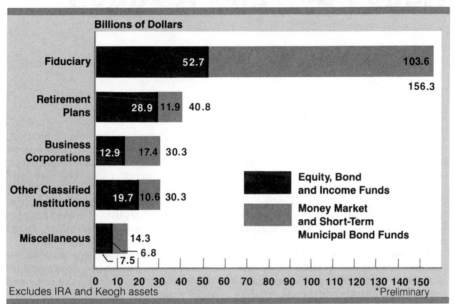

Billions of Dollars

	Equity, Bond and Income Funds	Money Market and Short-Term Municipal Bond Funds	Total
Fiduciary	52.7	103.6	156.3
Retirement Plans	28.9	11.9	40.8
Business Corporations	12.9	17.4	30.3
Other Classified Institutions	19.7	10.6	30.3
Miscellaneous	7.5	6.8	14.3

0 10 20 30 40 50 60 70 80 90 100 110 120 130 140 150

Excludes IRA and Keogh assets   *Preliminary

assets at the end of 1987. Money market institutional assets rose from $103.2 billion to $123.5 billion between 1986 and 1987.

The outstanding value of assets invested by institutions in stock, bond, and income funds rose in 1987 to $121.7 billion, up from $117.0 billion at yearend 1986. Total assets of the funds increased at a greater rate, however, which resulted in a modest decline in the share of assets held by institutions. At the end of 1987, 26.8 percent of total assets were held by institutions, down slightly from the 27.6 percent share they represented at the end of 1986.

Those institutional assets in money market funds were primarily in fiduciary accounts, business corporations, retirement plans, insurance companies, and other financial institutions. The increased assets in equity, bond, and income funds are concentrated in these four categories as well.

The number of institutional accounts has expanded over the years along with the rise in assets. In 1960, there were only about 347,000 accounts on the books. At the end of 1987, institutional accounts totaled 7.6 million. Since many of these are pooled accounts, the number of fund customers linked to institutions is even larger.

The institutional market is complex and includes a number of submarkets, each of which has many unique characteristics. By far, the largest such market is the fiduciary group.

At the end of 1987, fiduciary accounts of all types of funds numbered about 4.1 million and had an estimated total value of $156.3 billion.

The fiduciary market is composed of at least two broad segments: bank trusts, and individuals serving as trustees, guardians, and administrators. The former market is served mainly by the money market funds, while the latter is primarily the province of all other types of funds. This distinction is evident from the fact that the average-size fiduciary account associated with money market funds is much larger than stock, bond, and income funds.

Other statistical details relating to the institutional market are contained in tables presented in the data section of the Fact Book.

Regulation and Taxation

Mutual fund organizations are the most strictly regulated business entities under the federal securities laws. A former chairman of the United States Securities and Exchange Commission (SEC) said, "No issuer of securities is subject to more detailed regulation than mutual funds."

The laws governing mutual funds require exhaustive disclosure to the SEC, state regulators, and fund shareholders and entail continuous regulation of fund operations. Appropriately, however, these laws do not include supervision of the investment judgment of each fund's management.

Four major federal statutes regulate mutual funds.

The Securities Act of 1933 requires the filing of full information regarding the fund with the SEC. In addition, the 1933 act requires the fund to provide potential investors with a current prospectus. The prospectus makes detailed disclosures about the fund's management, its investment policies, objectives, and other essential data. The 1933 act also limits the types of advertisements which may be used by a mutual fund.

The purchase and sale of mutual fund shares, as with all securities, are subject to the anti-fraud provisions of the Securities Exchange Act of 1934.

The Investment Advisers Act of 1940 regulates the activities of investment advisers to mutual funds.

Most importantly, the mutual fund must register with the SEC under the Investment Company Act of 1940, which is a highly detailed regulatory statute. The 1940 act contains numerous provisions designed to prevent self-dealing and other conflicts of interest, maintain the integrity of fund assets, and prevent the fund and its shareholders from paying excessive fees and charges.

In addition to these federal statutes, most states regulate mutual funds whose shares are offered in those states.

Federal and state laws provide for appropriate disclosure to investors when it comes to potential returns and risks associated with individual funds. These laws are designed to ensure that mutual funds are operated and managed in the interests of their shareholders.

Taxation of Shareholders: Traditionally, an extra layer of taxation is avoided under the "conduit theory." Mutual fund shareholders are generally treated as if they directly held the securities in the fund's portfolio. Under Subchapter M of the Internal Revenue Code of 1954, qualified funds pay no federal income tax on their earnings and capital gains which are distributed to shareholders.

In order to qualify, a mutual fund has to distribute at least 90 percent of its investment company taxable income to its shareholders each year, among other requirements. Thus, a shareholder receives dividends and capital gain distributions from a qualifying fund without any tax being levied on the fund. Instead, shareholders report these payments on their own tax returns and pay the appropriate tax.

The Tax Reform Act of 1986 and subsequent legislation require a fund to distribute 97 percent of its income from dividends and interest, and 98 percent of its net realized capital gains with respect to the calendar year in which they are earned or realized. The 1986 act also requires shareholders to be taxed on their share of a fund's gross income (income before fund expenses are subtracted), rather than on net distributions, beginning in 1987. This change would have imposed a tax on the "phantom income" imputed to shareholders, that is, income that shareholders never received but for which they were held accountable on their tax returns. However, in 1987, Congress ameliorated this harsh treatment by enacting legislation to delay the imposition of the phantom income tax on mutual fund shareholders for one year.

Mutual Fund IRA Owners

The mutual fund industry has benefited substantially from the liberalized IRA program. Funds represented about 22 percent of the total IRA market at the end of 1987—up from about 10 percent at the beginning of 1982, the year in which Congress enabled all working Americans to establish IRAs.

The 1988 "IRA season," however, was conducted in a new tax environment that has modified the IRA marketplace. Furthermore, the stock market break of October 1987 may also affect the investment choices of fund IRA owners. These prospects make it more important than ever to identify the characteristics of fund IRA owners and establish a benchmark for future comparisons.

The characteristics of shareholders who own fund IRAs and those who do not were compiled from the Institute's 1986 shareholder survey. The data suggest that fund IRA owners constitute a distinct segment of the fund market. As shown in the accompanying table, fund IRA owners are younger than those who do not own fund IRAs, but not so young that retirement is a remote financial objective. Most fund IRA owners are still working and, consequently, their household incomes are higher than those not owning fund IRAs, most of whom are retired. Fund IRA owners have fewer household financial assets than shareholders who do not have fund IRAs, largely because they are younger and have had less time to accumulate them.

Characteristics of Shareholders* Owning Fund IRAs

Shareholder Characteristics**	Own Fund IRAs	Do Not Own Fund IRAs
Age	50.4 Yrs.	65.6 Yrs.
Household Income	$51,500	$39,400
Household Financial Assets (Excluding Real Estate)	$110,800	$150,300
Completed Graduate School	35.5%	26.2%
Male Financial Decisionmakers	77.3%	68.2%
Employed	77.1%	36.2%
Married	77.6%	64.8%
City/Suburban	79.3%	76.1%
Moderate Risk Takers	66.9%	42.1%

*"Shareholders" refers to the primary financial decisionmaker in households owning funds.
**Median except where noted.

Other characteristics of shareholders with fund IRAs include a greater tendency to have attained a graduate degree than shareholders who do not have fund IRAs, and a greater tendency to accept a moderate degree of risk when investing. Fund IRA owners are also more often male and married than nonowners, and they tend to reside in urbanized areas more than shareholders who do not own fund IRAs.

The reasons given by fund IRA owners for selecting funds instead of nonfund investments suggest that they are relatively sophisticated regarding their investments, and base their decisions on both quantitative and qualitative features of the product. On the other hand, shareholders who do not own fund IRAs (but who may own nonfund IRAs) appear to be less knowledgeable and possibly less experienced with funds, and rely more on reputation and word-of-mouth advice. This group of shareholders places less importance on product features in general.

The sharp contrast in investment decisionmaking between these two groups of shareholders is illustrated in the accompanying table. Fund IRA owners ranked the availability and quality of services as the most important considerations, with diversification, ease of investing, and higher returns as other important reasons for selecting a fund over a nonfund investment. Fund shareholders who do not own fund IRAs ranked the recommendations of friends, relatives, and personal acquaintances as the most important reason for selecting a mutual fund instead of a nonfund investment, followed by salespersons' recommendations, the safety of funds, and the fund company's reputation.

The survey also found that many shareholders have both fund and nonfund IRAs. In fact, 47 percent of all fund IRA owners also have a nonfund IRA. As can be seen in the accompanying table, the characteristics of these shareholders differ from the characteristics of shareholders who have only fund IRAs. Owners of both fund and

Main Reasons for Selecting a Fund IRA Instead of a Nonfund IRA

Fund IRA Owners	Shareholders Who Do Not Own Fund IRAs
1. More Services	1. Recommended by Friends, Relatives
2. Better Quality of Services	2. Recommended by a Salesperson
3. More Diversified Investments	3. Did Not Consider Nonfund Investments
4. Easier to Invest in	4. Safer Investment
5. Higher Investment Returns	5. Fund Companies Have Better Reputations

nonfund IRAs are generally younger and have substantially larger accumulations of household financial assets than owners of fund IRAs alone. They are somewhat less likely to have graduate degrees and are slightly more likely to be female. They also have higher household incomes, which can be attributed to the larger percentage of these shareholders who are married with two incomes—spouses of shareholders with both fund and nonfund IRAs are employed 57 percent of the time as compared to 53 percent for spouses of shareholders with fund IRAs only.

Many shareholders who have their IRAs invested in both nonfund products and funds are diversifying their retirement investments. Others, however, most likely bought nonfund IRAs from familiar sources such as local depository institutions soon after the rules covering who could open an IRA were liberalized. Only later, after becoming more knowledgeable about alternative IRA investments and more aware of the potential for higher returns from stock and bond funds, did they purchase fund IRAs.

Characteristics of Shareholders*
Who Own Both Fund and Nonfund IRAs

Shareholder Characteristics**	Own Both Fund and Nonfund IRAs	Own Only Fund IRAs
Age	52.6 Yrs.	59.9 Yrs.
Household Income	$53,500	$48,600
Household Financial Assets (Excluding Real Estate)	$132,600	$98,700
Completed Graduate School	33.5%	36.6%
Male Financial Decisionmakers	75.5%	77.8%
Married	81.1%	73.6%
City/Suburban	79.2%	78.8%
First Invested in Funds Prior to 1980	50.9%	52.1%

*"Shareholders" refers to the primary financial decisionmaker in households owning funds.
**Median except where noted.

Regional Markets for Mutual Funds

As mutual fund sales and assets expand, the awareness and ownership of funds also increase among consumers. From 1982 to 1987, the rise in the number of shareholder accounts was more than 150 percent. That growth rate was due to purchases from investors who were new to mutual funds, as well as to the repeat purchases of shareholders expanding their mutual fund portfolios.

Research by the Investment Company Institute identified the major characteristics of mutual fund shareholders based on a large-scale survey in 1986. Analysis of this database by geographic location of shareholder households presents these characteristics in a new and useful dimension—the regional markets for mutual funds.

There are measurable differences in mutual fund owners among locations in the United States and regional differences in comparison to the national profile of all shareholders. As seen in the accompanying chart, a comparison of the percentages of fund assets allocated among the four major regions of the United States does not show great differences. However, when the top ten states are examined by asset level, some considerable differences in total fund assets held by residents of the states appear.

The characteristics of the types of people who own mutual funds within each of the states also vary. The data shows for example that the average mutual fund shareholder is older in the state of Florida than in other areas. This finding corresponds to census statistics which indicate that a large number of residents in this state are over 65 years of age.

Total Fund Assets By U.S. Region 1986

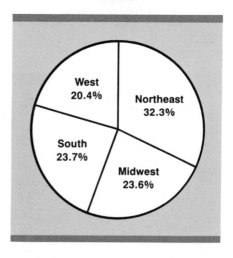

West 20.4%
Northeast 32.3%
South 23.7%
Midwest 23.6%

Shareholders in many states present a different profile from the national profile. Texas is a good example of a state in which the median age of the shareholder is significantly lower than the national median age. In comparison with the other nine top states, the household income in Texas is measurably higher, and the median amount invested in mutual funds is lower than in many other of the top states listed.

The regional survey also uncovered the following facts:

• Of the total assets in 1986, the highest regional figure is for the Northeast, particularly in the Middle Atlantic division (New York, New Jersey, Pennsylvania). California has the highest fund asset level of all states.

• In general, mutual fund shareholders are well-educated; 34 percent of them have completed graduate school. Among states, this figure is highest in Illinois (39 percent).

• Thirty-two percent of United States shareholders are retired. In the South Atlantic states, this figure is 41 percent, and in the state of Florida alone 62 percent of mutual fund shareholders are retired.

• Median income for shareholder households is highest in the West South Central division ($57,400). The fund owner median income level in Texas is the highest of the top ten states at $56,800. The table shows that median income is lowest for shareholders in the state of Pennsylvania at $39,000.

• The median amount that mutual fund owners have invested per household in mutual funds is highest in the South Atlantic division ($43,000) and lowest in the Pacific division ($33,100). State comparisons also show that shareholders in Florida have a median amount of $55,500 invested in mutual funds while California shareholders have a much lower median amount of $33,500 invested.

• The median age of mutual fund shareholders is highest at 58 in the West North Central division. Florida has the highest median shareholder age at 65 years and Texas shareholders are the youngest with a median age of 46 years.

Characteristics of Fund Shareholders by State*
(1986)

	Median Age	Median Household Income	Median Amount Invested In Funds	Percent Of Total Fund Assets
California	56.5	$47,100	$33,500	12.5%
New York	53.0	48,600	41,700	11.7
New Jersey	52.8	54,300	40,400	6.7
Florida	64.5	42,300	55,500	5.9
Illinois	49.8	50,600	39,300	5.9
Pennsylvania	55.7	39,000	36,000	5.5
Massachusetts	55.4	43,600	40,900	4.8
Texas	45.6	56,800	35,700	4.1
Ohio	55.5	39,800	34,600	3.6
Michigan	54.6	47,800	33,900	3.2
All Survey Respondents	52.4	$46,400	$37,500	100.0%

*"Shareholders" refers to the primary financial decisionmaker in households owning funds.
States listed here represent the top ten states in 1986 assets of mutual funds.

Glossary of Mutual Fund Terms

(For explanation of types of funds, see pages 8–9; for retirement plans, see page 44.)

Adviser

The organization employed by a mutual fund to give professional advice on the fund's investments and asset management practices (also called "investment adviser").

Asked or Offering Price
(As seen in some mutual fund newspaper listings.) The price at which a mutual fund's shares can be purchased. The asked or offering price means the current net asset value per share plus sales charge, if any.

Automatic Reinvestment

An option available to mutual fund shareholders in which fund dividends and capital gains distributions are automatically plowed back into the fund to buy new shares and thereby increase holdings.

Bid or Redemption Price
(As seen in some mutual fund newspaper listings.) The price at which a mutual fund's shares are redeemed (bought back) by the fund. The bid or redemption price usually equals the current net asset value per share.

Broker/Dealer (or Dealer)

A firm that buys and sells mutual fund shares and other securities to the public.

Capital Gains Distributions

Payments to mutual fund shareholders of profits realized on the sale of securities in the fund's portfolio. These amounts are usually distributed to shareholders annually.

Capital Growth

An increase in market value of a mutual fund's securities, as reflected in the net asset value of fund shares. This is a long-term objective of many mutual funds.

Closed-End Investment Company

Unlike mutual funds (known as "open-end" investment companies), closed-end companies issue a limited number of shares and do not redeem them (buy them back). Instead, closed-end shares are traded in the securities markets, with supply and demand determining the price.

Contractual Plan

A program for the accumulation of mutual fund shares in which the investor agrees to invest a fixed amount on a regular basis for a specified number of years. A substantial portion of the sales charge applicable to the total investment is usually deducted from early payments.

Custodian

The organization (usually a bank) that keeps custody of securities and other assets of a mutual fund.

Diversification

The mutual fund policy of spreading its investments among a number of different securities to reduce the risks inherent in investing. The average investor would find it difficult to amass a portfolio as diversified as that of a mutual fund.

55

Dollar-Cost Averaging

Investing equal amounts of money at regular intervals regardless of whether securities markets are moving up or down. This practice reduces average share costs to the investor who acquires more shares in periods of lower securities prices and fewer shares in periods of higher prices. Unlike a contractual plan, dollar-cost averaging is voluntary.

Exchange Privilege

Enables mutual fund shareholders to transfer their investment from one fund to another within the same fund family as shareholder needs or objectives change. Usually funds let investors use the exchange privilege several times a year for a low or no fee per exchange.

Income Dividends

Payments to mutual fund shareholders of dividends, interest, and/or short-term capital gains earned on the fund's portfolio of securities after deducting operating expenses.

Investment Adviser

See Adviser.

Investment Company

A corporation, trust, or partnership which invests pooled funds of shareholders in securities appropriate to the fund's objective. Among the benefits of investment companies are professional management and diversification. Mutual funds ("open-end" investment companies) are the most popular type of investment company.

Investment Objective

The goal—such as long-term capital growth, current income, growth, growth and income, etc.—which an investor or a mutual fund pursues. Each fund's objective is stated in its prospectus.

Long-Term Funds

An industry designation for all funds other than short-term funds (money market and short-term municipal bond). The two broad categories of long-term funds are equity (stock) and bond and income funds.

Management Fee

The amount paid by mutual funds to their investment advisers. The average annual fee industrywide is about one-half of one percent of fund assets.

Mutual Fund

An investment company that pools money from shareholders and invests in a variety of securities, including stocks, bonds, and money market securities. A mutual fund stands ready to buy back (redeem) its shares at their current net asset value. The value of the shares depends on the market value of the fund's portfolio securities at the time. Most mutual funds offer new shares continuously.

Net Asset Value Per Share

The market worth of a mutual fund's total assets–securities, cash, and any accrued earnings—after deducting liabilities, divided by the number of shares outstanding.

Open-End Investment Company

The statutory terminology for a mutual fund, indicating that it stands ready to redeem (buy back) its shares on demand.

Over-The-Counter Market

The market for securities transactions conducted through a communications network connecting dealers in stocks and bonds. The rules of such trading are written and enforced by the National Association of Securities Dealers, Inc. (NASD), the same organization that provides self-policing of member firms in the distribution of mutual fund shares.

Payroll Deduction Plan

An arrangement some employers offer whereby employees may accumulate shares in a mutual fund. Employees authorize their employer to deduct a specified amount from their salary at stated times and transfer the proceeds to the fund.

Periodic Payment Plan
See Contractual Plan

Prospectus
The official booklet that describes a mutual fund. The prospectus contains information as required by the U.S. Securities and Exchange Commission on such subjects as the fund's investment objectives and policies, services, investment restrictions, officers and directors, how shares are bought and redeemed, fund fees and other charges, and the fund's financial statements.

Redemption Price
The amount per share that mutual fund shareholders receive when they liquidate their shares (also known as the "bid price").

Reinvestment Privilege
A service provided by most mutual funds for the automatic reinvestment of shareholder dividends and capital gains distributions into additional shares.

Sales Charge
An amount charged to purchase shares in many mutual funds sold by brokers or other members of a sales force. Typically, the charge ranges from 4 to 8.5 percent of the initial investment. The charge is added to the net asset value per share when determining the offering price.

Short-Term Funds
An industry designation for money market and short-term municipal bond funds. Due to the special nature of these funds and the huge, continuous inflows and outflows of money they experience, they are rarely viewed in terms of sales figures, as long-term funds are. Tracking changes in total assets is usually the preferred method of following trends in short-term funds.

Transfer Agent
The organization employed by a mutual fund to prepare and maintain records relating to the accounts of its shareholders.

12b-1 Fee
Fee charged by some funds and named after the 1980 Securities and Exchange Commission rule that permits them. Such fees pay for distribution costs such as advertising or for commissions paid to brokers. The fund's prospectus details 12b-1 charges, if applicable.

Underwriter
The organization that acts as the distributor of a mutual fund's shares to broker/dealers and investors.

Unit Investment Trust
An investment company that purchases a fixed portfolio of income-producing securities. Units in the trust are sold to investors by brokers.

Variable Annuity
An investment contract sold to an investor by an insurance company. Capital is accumulated, often through investment in a mutual fund, and converted to an income stream at a future date, perhaps retirement. Income payments vary with the value of the account.

Withdrawal Plans
A program in which shareholders receive payments from their mutual fund investments at regular intervals. Typically, these payments are drawn from the fund's dividends and capital gains distributions, if any, and from principal, as needed. Many mutual funds offer these plans.

Data

Table of Contents

Section V:
Retirement Plans

Section VI:

Institutional Investors

An Overview

Accounts

Assets

Total Industry Assets
(Billions of Dollars)

	Equity, Bond, and Income Funds	Money Market Funds and Short-Term Municipal Bond Funds	Total
1975	$ 42.2	$ 3.7	$ 45.9
1976	47.6	3.7	51.3
1977	45.0	3.9	48.9
1978	45.0	10.9	55.9
1979	49.0	45.2	94.2
1980	58.4	76.3	134.7
1981	55.2	186.1	241.3
1982	76.8	219.8	296.6
1983	113.6	179.3	292.9
1984	137.1	233.5	370.6
1985	251.7	243.8	495.5
1986	424.2	292.1	716.3
1987	453.8	316.1	769.9

Total Industry Shareholder Accounts

(Millions)

Year	Equity, Bond, and Income Funds	Money Market Funds and Short-Term Municipal Bond Funds	Total
1975	9.7	0.2	9.9
1976	8.9	0.2	9.1
1977	8.5	0.2	8.7
1978	8.2	0.5	8.7
1979	7.5	2.3	9.8
1980	7.3	4.8	12.1
1981	7.2	10.3	17.5
1982	8.2	13.2	21.4
1983	12.1	12.5	24.6
1984	14.4	13.8	28.2
1985	20.0	15.0	35.0
1986	29.8	16.3	46.1
1987	37.0	17.7	54.7

Total Number of Funds

	Equity, Bond, and Income Funds	Money Market Funds and Short-Term Municipal Bond Funds	Total
1975	390	36	426
1976	404	48	452
1977	427	50	477
1978	444	61	505
1979	448	76	524
1980	458	106	564
1981	486	179	665
1982	539	318	857
1983	653	373	1,026
1984	820	426	1,246
1985	1,071	460	1,531
1986	1,356	487	1,843
1987	1,781	543	2,324

An Overview:
Shareholder Accounts,
Total Net Assets, and Liquid Assets
Equity, Bond, and Income Funds
1970–1987

Calendar Yearend	Number of Reporting Funds	Number of Accounts (Thousands)	Net Assets (Billions of Dollars)	Liquid Assets (Billions of Dollars)
1970	361	10,690.3	$ 47.6	$ 3.1
1971	392	10,901.0	55.0	2.6
1972	410	10,635.3	59.8	2.6
1973	421	10,330.9	46.5	3.4
1974	416	9,970.4	34.1	3.4
1975	390	9,712.5	42.2	3.2
1976	404	8,879.4	47.6	2.4
1977	427	8,515.1	45.0	3.3
1978	444	8,190.6	45.0	4.5
1979	446	7,482.2	49.0	4.7
1980	458	7,325.5	58.4	5.3
1981	486	7,175.5	55.2	5.3
1982	539	8,190.3	76.8	6.0
1983	653	12,065.0	113.6	8.3
1984	820	14,471.3	137.1	12.2
1985	1,071	19,845.6	251.7	20.6
1986	1,356	29,790.2R	424.2	30.7
1987	1,781	36,971.1	453.8	38.0

NOTE: Figures for shareholder accounts represent combined totals for member companies. Duplications have not been eliminated.

R—Revised

Comparable data for short-term funds can be found on page 86. Industry totals can be found on pages 62-64.

Type of Shareholder Accounts
Equity, Bond, and Income Funds
1971–1987
(Thousands)

Yearend	Total Shareholder Accounts	Regular Accounts	Contractual Accumulation Plans	Contractual Single Payment Plans	Withdrawal Accounts
Number					
1971	10,901	8,996	1,455	169	281
1972	10,635	8,856	1,342	157	280
1973	10,331	8,699	1,214	166	252
1974	9,970	8,524	1,081	140	225
1975	9,667	8,302	1,029	126	210
1976	8,879	7,647	930	112	190
1977	8,515	7,395	844	101	175
1978	8,068	7,080	757	75	156
1979	7,482	6,602	677	64	139
1980	7,326	6,598	554	45	129
1981	7,175	6,486	537	30	122
1982	8,190	7,573	471	28	118
1983	12,065	11,326	585	20	134
1984	14,424	13,666	615	17	126
1985	19,846	19,008	647	17	174
1986	29,790R	28,919R	624	16	231
1987	36,971	36,003	687	17	264
Percent					
1971	100.0%	82.5%	13.3%	1.6%	2.6%
1972	100.0	83.3	12.6	1.5	2.6
1973	100.0	84.2	11.8	1.6	2.4
1974	100.0	85.5	10.8	1.4	2.3
1975	100.0	85.9	10.6	1.3	2.2
1976	100.0	86.1	10.5	1.3	2.1
1977	100.0	86.9	9.9	1.2	2.0
1978	100.0	87.8	9.4	0.9	1.9
1979	100.0	88.2	9.0	0.9	1.9
1980	100.0	90.1	7.6	0.6	1.7
1981	100.0	90.4	7.5	0.4	1.7
1982	100.0	92.5	5.8	0.3	1.4
1983	100.0	93.8	4.9	0.2	1.1
1984	100.0	94.8	4.2	0.1	0.9
1985	100.0	95.8	3.2	0.1	0.9
1986	100.0	97.0	2.1	0.1	0.8
1987	100.0	97.4	1.8	0.1	0.7

R—Revised

Total Net Assets of Equity, Bond, and Income Funds by Fund Characteristics

Yearend (Millions of Dollars)

	1986 Dollars	1986 Percent	1987 Dollars	1987 Percent
TOTAL NET ASSETS	**$424,156.4**	**100.0%**	**$453,842.4**	**100.0%**
Method of Sale				
Sales Force	$ 304,637.3	71.8%	$ 331,752.8	73.1%
Direct Marketing	107,911.3	25.4	107,496.1	23.7
Variable Annuity	9,274.3	2.2	12,730.1	2.8
Not Offering Shares	2,333.5	0.6	1,863.4	0.4
Investment Objective				
Aggressive Growth	$ 25,006.9	5.9%	$ 27,298.1	6.0%
Growth	43,579.5	10.3	48,037.6	10.6
Growth & Income	55,944.1	13.2	64,032.5	14.1
Precious Metals	2,027.0	0.5	4,050.9	0.9
International	7,186.1	1.7	6,982.3	1.5
Global Equity	8,282.0	2.0	10,449.2	2.3
Flexible Portfolio	1,461.8	0.3	4,287.2	1.0
Balanced	7,483.0	1.8	9,024.7	2.0
Income-Equity	12,560.1	3.0	14,745.1	3.3
Income-Mixed	10,323.7	2.4	11,418.4	2.5
Income-Bond	11,417.9	2.7	12,580.0	2.8
Option/Income	6,952.9	1.6	5,095.2	1.1
U.S. Government Income	82,444.2	19.4	88,906.2	19.6
Ginnie Mae	39,619.9	9.3	34,204.0	7.5
Global Bond	523.2	0.1	2,137.1	0.5
Corporate Bond	9,080.5	2.1	9,470.5	2.1
High-Yield Bond	24,591.6	5.8	24,157.2	5.3
Long-Term Municipal Bond	49,857.2	11.8	49,174.6	10.8
Long-Term State Municipal Bond	25,814.8	6.1	27,791.6	6.1

Liquid Assets of Equity, Bond, and Income Funds by Fund Characteristics

Yearend (Millions of Dollars)

	1986 Dollars	1986 Percent	1987 Dollars	1987 Percent
NET CASH & EQUIVALENT	**$30,716.3**	**100.0%**	**$38,006.1**	**100.0%**
Method of Sale				
Sales Force	$ 23,150.6	75.4%	$ 28,559.4	75.1%
Direct Marketing	6,343.3	20.6	7,856.6	20.7
Variable Annuity	1,048.4	3.4	1,438.7	3.8
Not Offering Shares	174.0	0.6	151.4	0.4
Investment Objective				
Aggressive Growth	$ 1,596.8	5.2%	$ 2,515.6	6.6%
Growth	4,517.7	14.7	5,216.5	13.7
Growth & Income	5,860.4	19.1	5,124.7	13.5
Precious Metals	82.3	0.3	380.3	1.0
International	396.1	1.3	352.9	0.9
Global Equity	1,063.9	3.5	1,643.9	4.3
Flexible Portfolio	182.5	0.6	814.0	2.1
Balanced	706.3	2.3	843.1	2.2
Income-Equity	1,138.4	3.7	1,086.1	2.9
Income-Mixed	838.4	2.7	883.9	2.3
Income-Bond	1,226.7	4.0	1,407.4	3.7
Option/Income	845.3	2.7	261.7	0.7
U.S. Government Income	7,772.4	25.3	8,847.8	23.3
Ginnie Mae	438.6	1.4	1,258.3	3.3
Global Bond	110.3	0.3	474.2	1.3
Corporate Bond	572.7	1.9	749.8	2.0
High-Yield Bond	1,224.7	4.0	1,760.0	4.6
Long-Term Municipal Bond	1,501.4	4.9	3,184.5	8.4
Long-Term State Municipal Bond	641.4	2.1	1,201.4	3.2

Total Net Assets of Mutual Funds by Investment Objective Within Method of Sales

1984–1987

(Millions of Dollars)

Sales Force

	1984	1985	1986	1987
Aggressive Growth	$ 6,626.0	$ 8,107.2	$ 9,024.4	$ 10,088.6
Growth	17,624.5	22,479.9	28,245.5	30,940.1
Growth & Income	17,751.3	24,156.3	34,262.1	38,985.8
Precious Metals	180.2	975.4	1,223.9	2,415.7
International	272.6	701.1	2,097.0	2,608.0
Global Equity	3,786.6	5,172.8	7,944.1	10,248.3
Flexible Portfolio	638.3	853.3	1,213.8	3,720.9
Balanced	2,044.0	2,807.0	5,376.4	6,136.0
Income-Equity	1,627.1	2,718.3	5,478.9	6,321.7
Income-Mixed	3,222.2	5,283.5	8,054.1	9,179.0
Income-Bond	2,541.6	3,793.1	7,433.9	8,633.2
Option/Income	3,255.4	5,493.5	6,835.1	4,863.3
U.S. Government Income	6,339.4	39,092.3	78,838.7	86,069.3
Ginnie Mae	3,600.9	15,715.7	31,866.6	27,490.3
Global Bond	34.3	64.4	453.2	1,589.2
Corporate Bond	2,935.2	4,294.0	7,735.6	8,055.6
High-Yield Bond	6,471.3	11,025.5	19,612.3	19,922.6
Long-Term Municipal Bond	8,073.1	15,273.6	29,782.6	32,782.7
Long-Term State Municipal Bond	3,607.0	8,404.9	19,159.2	21,702.5
Total	**$ 90,631.0**	**$176,411.8**	**$304,637.4**	**$331,752.8**

Direct Marketing

	1984	1985	1986	1987
Aggressive Growth	$ 7,367.8	$ 11,482.1	$ 15,321.1	$ 16,527.7
Growth	7,515.8	9,928.6	11,633.2	12,604.7
Growth & Income	9,406.5	13,525.8	18,333.5	19,810.6
Precious Metals	195.4	522.4	801.7	1,632.3
International	896.5	1,785.0	5,089.2	4,355.5
Global Equity	0.0	0.0	41.0	190.3
Flexible Portfolio	11.5	34.1	175.5	370.4
Balanced	859.7	1,266.7	2,070.6	2,780.2
Income-Equity	2,423.3	4,004.8	7,078.5	8,393.3
Income-Mixed	863.1	1,653.9	2,038.0	2,044.3
Income-Bond	1,287.9	2,048.9	3,195.2	3,051.4
Option/Income	82.5	108.6	111.5	226.2
U.S. Government Income	266.4	1,152.0	3,132.2	2,242.6
Ginnie Mae	324.4	1,892.7	7,164.4	6,044.3
Global Bond	0.0	0.0	70.0	547.9
Corporate Bond	333.4	486.0	886.5	951.0
High-Yield Bond	641.5	1,905.9	4,039.0	3,242.2
Long-Term Municipal Bond	7,934.1	12,651.1	20,074.6	16,392.0
Long-Term State Municipal Bond	1,175.5	3,114.6	6,655.6	6,089.2
Total	**$ 41,585.3**	**$ 67,563.2**	**$107,911.3**	**$107,496.1**

Distribution of Mutual Fund Assets in Equity, Bond, and Income Funds Yearend, 1970–1987

(Millions of Dollars)

Year	Total Net Assets	Net Cash & Equivalent	Corporate Bonds	Preferred Stocks	Common Stocks	Municipal Bonds	Long-Term U.S. Gov't.	Other
1970	$47,618	$3,124	$4,286	$1,143	$38,540	NA	NA	$525
1971	55,045	2,601	4,910	1,206	45,891	NA	NA	437
1972	59,831	2,598	5,068	993	50,735	NA	NA	437
1973	46,519	3,426	4,196	623	37,698	NA	NA	576
1974	34,062	3,357	3,611	426	26,103	NA	NA	565
1975	42,179	3,209	4,766	506	33,158	NA	NA	540
1976	47,582	2,352	6,977	655	37,158	NA	NA	440
1977	45,049	3,274	6,475	418	30,746	$2,256	$1,295	585
1978	44,980	4,507	5,545	405	30,678	2,550	1,093	202
1979	48,980	4,995	5,582	443	34,334	2,651	798	177
1980	58,400	5,321	6,582	531	41,561	2,866	1,433	106
1981	55,207	5,277	7,489	399	36,649	3,046	2,147	200
1982	76,841	6,040	10,833	1,628	47,720	6,797	3,752	71
1983	113,599	8,343	13,052	1,474	72,942	13,368	3,894	526
1984	137,126	11,978	15,018	1,627	81,597	18,522	8,009	375
1985	251,695	20,607	24,961	3,773	119,698	38,339	43,471	846
1986	424,156	30,716	47,310	7,387	153,657	70,875	111,536	2,675
1987	453,842	38,006	41,661	5,566	176,372	68,578	119,854	3,805

Percent

Year	Total Net Assets	Net Cash & Equivalent	Corporate Bonds	Preferred Stocks	Common Stocks	Municipal Bonds	Long-Term U.S. Gov't.	Other
1970	100.0%	6.6%	9.0%	2.4%	80.9%	NA	NA	1.1%
1971	100.0	4.7	8.9	2.2	83.4	NA	NA	0.8
1972	100.0	4.3	8.5	1.7	84.8	NA	NA	0.7
1973	100.0	7.4	9.0	1.2	81.0	NA	NA	1.3
1974	100.0	9.9	10.6	1.2	76.6	NA	NA	1.7
1975	100.0	7.6	11.3	1.2	78.6	NA	NA	1.3
1976	100.0	4.9	14.7	1.4	78.1	NA	NA	0.9
1977	100.0	7.3	14.4	0.9	68.2	5.0%	2.9%	1.3
1978	100.0	10.0	12.3	0.9	68.2	5.7	2.4	0.5
1979	100.0	10.2	11.4	0.9	70.1	5.4	1.6	0.4
1980	100.0	9.1	11.3	0.9	71.2	4.9	2.4	0.2
1981	100.0	9.5	13.6	0.7	66.4	5.5	3.9	0.4
1982	100.0	7.9	14.1	2.1	62.1	8.8	4.9	0.1
1983	100.0	7.3	11.5	1.3	64.2	11.8	3.4	0.5
1984	100.0	8.7	11.0	1.2	59.5	13.5	5.8	0.3
1985	100.0	8.2	9.9	1.5	47.6	15.2	17.3	0.3
1986	100.0	7.3	11.2	1.7	36.2	16.7	26.3	0.6
1987	100.0	8.4	9.2	1.2	38.9	15.1	26.4	0.8

An Overview: Sales, Redemptions, and Net Sales of Equity, Bond, and Income Funds

1970–1987

(Millions of Dollars)

Year	Sales	Redemptions	Net Sales
1970	$4,625.8	$2,987.6	$1,638.2
1971	5,147.2	4,750.2	397.0
1972	4,892.5	6,562.9	(1,670.4)
1973	4,359.3	5,651.1	(1,291.8)
1974	3,091.5	3,380.9	(289.4)
1975	3,307.2	3,686.3	(379.1)
1976	4,360.5	6,801.2	(2,440.7)
1977	6,399.6	6,026.0	373.6
1978	6,705.3	7,232.4	(527.1)
1979	6,826.1	8,005.0	(1,178.9)
1980	9,993.7	8,200.0	1,793.7
1981	9,710.4	7,470.4	2,240.0
1982	15,738.3	7,571.8	8,166.5
1983	40,325.1	14,677.6	25,647.5
1984	45,856.8	20,030.1	25,826.7
1985	114,313.5	33,763.3	80,550.2
1986	215,847.9	67,012.7	148,835.2
1987	190,604.7	116,224.3	74,380.4

Comparable data for short-term funds can be found on page 86.

Sales of Equity, Bond, and Income
Funds by Fund Characteristics
(Millions of Dollars)

	1986		1987	
	Dollars	**Percent**	**Dollars**	**Percent**
SALES	**$215,847.9**	**100.0%**	**$190,604.7**	**100.0%**
Type of Sales				
Regular Single Payment	$ 201,144.9	93.2%	$ 171,031.4	89.7%
Contractual Accumulation Plan	471.8	0.2	469.3	0.2
Contractual Single Payment	229.5	0.1	118.5	0.1
Reinvested Investment Income	14,001.7	6.5	18,985.5	10.0
Method of Sales				
Sales Force	$ 161,577.6	74.9%	$ 132,015.5	69.3%
Direct Marketing	49,941.7	23.1	53,067.5	27.8
Variable Annuity	4,282.1	2.0	5,501.0	2.9
Not Offering Shares	46.5	0.0	20.7	0.0
Investment Objective				
Aggressive Growth	$ 9,928.2	4.6%	$ 11,732.5	6.2%
Growth	12,459.3	5.8	17,723.5	9.3
Growth & Income	18,811.0	8.7	23,320.2	12.2
Precious Metals	656.6	0.3	3,180.8	1.7
International	4,169.8	1.9	4,183.6	2.2
Global Equity	3,118.0	1.5	3,130.4	1.6
Flexible Portfolio	520.6	0.3	2,966.3	1.6
Balanced	3,341.0	1.6	3,263.4	1.7
Income-Equity	5,470.3	2.5	6,760.2	3.5
Income-Mixed	6,799.9	3.1	5,915.5	3.1
Income-Bond	5,435.5	2.5	5,400.6	2.8
Option/Income	3,103.5	1.4	2,011.1	1.1
U.S. Government Income	54,446.4	25.2	44,033.1	23.1
Ginnie Mae	28,860.2	13.4	13,251.1	7.0
Global Bond	439.2	0.2	1,118.7	0.6
Corporate Bond	4,430.1	2.1	3,683.5	1.9
High-Yield Bond	13,978.9	6.5	10,020.1	5.3
Long-Term Municipal Bond	24,660.0	11.4	17,991.2	9.4
Long-Term State Municipal Bond	15,219.4	7.0	10,918.9	5.7

Sales of Mutual Funds by Investment Objective Within Method of Sales
1984–1987
(Millions of Dollars)

Sales Force

	1984	1985	1986	1987
Aggressive Growth	$ 1,463.9	$ 1,517.5	$ 2,380.5	$ 4,077.6
Growth	3,505.1	4,751.2	7,697.4	10,508.8
Growth & Income	2,749.9	4,730.3	12,044.4	12,856.3
Precious Metals	81.0	223.5	204.6	1,277.5
International	149.7	198.8	1,048.5	1,988.8
Global Equity	969.1	1,088.3	3,088.5	3,076.4
Flexible Portfolio	85.4	138.1	344.5	2,610.9
Balanced	141.5	629.5	2,567.1	2,132.8
Income-Equity	338.9	1,104.6	2,640.6	3,175.3
Income-Mixed	1,611.6	3,197.6	5,335.9	4,723.4
Income-Bond	584.3	1,202.7	3,628.7	3,767.7
Option/Income	1,795.2	2,708.7	3,041.0	1,710.3
U.S. Government Income	5,849.6	35,654.5	51,624.5	42,050.7
Ginnie Mae	2,690.7	11,765.1	24,930.1	9,710.8
Global Bond	5.9	25.7	407.6	775.3
Corporate Bond	728.0	1,384.8	3,808.4	2,875.6
High-Yield Bond	2,061.8	4,665.3	10,541.5	7,012.8
Long-Term Municipal Bond	3,764.6	6,753.9	15,441.4	10,371.1
Long-Term State Municipal Bond	1,617.0	4,686.0	10,802.4	7,313.3
Total	**$ 30,193.2**	**$ 86,426.1**	**$161,577.6**	**$132,015.4**

Direct Marketing

	1984	1985	1986	1987
Aggressive Growth	$ 2,717.4	$ 5,125.3	$ 7,267.9	$ 7,285.9
Growth	1,550.8	2,050.2	3,624.6	5,723.8
Growth & Income	3,166.8	3,594.2	5,552.4	8,473.5
Precious Metals	166.5	385.3	452.0	1,900.5
International	450.7	562.3	3,121.4	2,192.6
Global Equity	0.0	0.3	22.6	50.3
Flexible Portfolio	9.0	30.2	142.6	232.4
Balanced	84.9	259.3	759.4	1,061.2
Income-Equity	661.6	1,179.5	2,829.5	3,584.2
Income-Mixed	457.7	733.1	1,345.9	1,112.1
Income-Bond	422.8	847.7	1,518.0	1,387.7
Option/Income	50.4	64.0	61.8	300.5
U.S. Government Income	87.6	884.8	2,554.6	1,702.4
Ginnie Mae	171.4	1,281.7	3,660.0	3,301.7
Global Bond	0.0	0.0	31.6	343.4
Corporate Bond	137.9	152.9	368.0	579.7
High-Yield Bond	320.1	1,051.1	2,993.7	2,610.1
Long-Term Municipal Bond	3,567.8	5,875.7	9,218.7	7,620.0
Long-Term State Municipal Bond	907.5	2,108.3	4,417.0	3,605.5
Total	**$ 14,930.9**	**$ 26,185.9**	**$ 49,941.7**	**$ 53,067.5**

Sales and Reinvested Dividends
by Fund Characteristics
1986–1987
(Millions of Dollars)

	Total Sales	Total Reinvested Dividends	Sales Less Reinvested Dividends
1986			
Total	**$215,847.9**	**$14,001.7**	**$201,846.2**
Method of Sales			
Sales Force	$161,577.6	$10,264.4	$151,313.2
Direct Marketing	49,941.7	3,514.1	46,427.6
Variable Annuity	4,282.1	200.1	4,082.0
Not Offering Shares	46.5	23.1	23.4
Investment Objective			
Aggressive Growth	$ 9,928.2	$ 336.8	$ 9,591.4
Growth	12,459.3	1,188.3	11,271.0
Growth & Income	18,811.0	1,714.1	17,096.9
Precious Metals	656.6	26.7	629.9
International	4,169.8	53.1	4,116.7
Global Equity	3,118.0	159.1	2,958.9
Flexible Portfolio	520.6	35.5	485.1
Balanced	3,341.0	215.3	3,125.7
Income-Equity	5,470.3	226.9	5,243.4
Income-Mixed	6,799.9	526.6	6,273.3
Income-Bond	5,435.5	529.9	4,905.6
Option/Income	3,103.5	322.2	2,781.3
U.S. Government Income	54,446.4	2,901.8	51,544.6
Ginnie Mae	28,860.2	1,413.6	27,446.6
Global Bond	439.2	7.4	431.8
Corporate Bond	4,430.1	364.3	4,065.8
High-Yield Bond	13,978.9	1,333.8	12,645.1
Long-Term Municipal Bond	24,660.0	1,931.8	22,728.2
Long-Term State Municipal Bond	15,219.4	714.5	14,504.9
1987			
Total	**$190,604.7**	**$18,985.5**	**$171,619.2**
Method of Sales			
Sales Force	$132,015.5	$14,297.5	$117,718.0
Direct Marketing	53,067.5	4,124.8	48,942.7
Variable Annuity	5,501.0	555.5	4,945.5
Not Offering Shares	20.7	7.7	13.0
Investment Objective			
Aggressive Growth	$ 11,732.5	$ 273.1	$ 11,459.4
Growth	17,723.5	1,675.1	16,048.4
Growth & Income	23,320.2	1,950.7	21,369.5
Precious Metals	3,180.8	85.3	3,095.5
International	4,183.6	179.6	4,004.0
Global Equity	3,130.4	305.7	2,824.7
Flexible Portfolio	2,966.3	178.3	2,788.0
Balanced	3,263.4	419.3	2,844.1
Income-Equity	6,760.2	342.4	6,417.8
Income-Mixed	5,915.5	607.9	5,307.6
Income-Bond	5,400.6	790.7	4,609.9
Option/Income	2,011.1	309.3	1,701.8
U.S. Government Income	44,033.1	4,509.0	39,524.1
Ginnie Mae	13,251.1	1,758.0	11,493.1
Global Bond	1,118.7	46.0	1,072.7
Corporate Bond	3,683.5	459.7	3,223.8
High-Yield Bond	10,020.1	1,735.6	8,284.5
Long-Term Municipal Bond	17,991.2	2,349.6	15,641.6
Long-Term State Municipal Bond	10,918.9	1,010.2	9,908.7

Equity, Bond, and Income Funds'
Distributions to Shareholders

(Millions of Dollars)

Year	Distributions From	
	Net Investment Income	Net Realized Capital Gains
1970	$1,414.1	$ 922.1
1971	1,330.7	775.5
1972	1,286.6	1,402.6
1973	1,300.2	943.3
1974	1,553.2	484.3
1975	1,449.1	219.2
1976	1,580.0	470.9
1977	1,789.7	634.8
1978	2,116.0	710.6
1979	2,451.4	929.9
1980	2,669.0	1,774.2
1981	3,143.0	2,697.2
1982	3,832.9	2,350.1
1983	4,981.0	4,391.6
1984	7,238.4	6,019.2
1985	12,864.2	4,984.6
1986	22,273.4	17,463.8
1987	31,823.7	22,975.6

Annual Redemption Rate
for Equity, Bond, and Income Funds
1970–1987
(Millions of Dollars)

Year	Average Total Net Assets	Redemptions	Redemption Rate
1970	$ 47,954	$ 2,988	6.2%
1971	51,332	4,750	9.3
1972	57,438	6,563	11.4
1973	53,175	5,651	10.6
1974	40,290	3,381	8.4
1975	38,120	3,686	9.7
1976	44,880	6,801	15.2
1977	46,316	6,026	13.0
1978	45,014	7,232	16.4
1979	46,980	8,005	17.0
1980	53,690	8,200	15.3
1981	56,803	7,470	13.2
1982	66,024	7,572	11.5
1983	95,220	14,678	15.4
1984	125,362	20,030	16.0
1985	194,411	33,763	17.4
1986	337,926	67,013	19.8
1987	438,999	116,224	26.5

NOTE: "Average" Value Assets are an average of values at the beginning of the year and at the end of the year. The redemption rate is the dollar redemption volume as a percent of average assets.

Redemptions of Equity, Bond, and Income Funds by Fund Characteristics

(Millions of Dollars)

	1986		1987	
	Dollars	**Percent**	**Dollars**	**Percent**
Redemptions	**$67,012.7**	**100.0%**	**$116,224.3**	**100.0%**
Type of Redemption				
Regular Account	$ 66,669.9	99.5%	$ 115,142.3	99.1%
Contractual Account	342.8	0.5	1,082.0	0.9
Method of Sales				
Sales Force	$ 45,927.9	68.5%	$ 81,528.4	70.1%
Direct Marketing	19,408.6	29.0	31,696.8	27.3
Variable Annuity	1,108.9	1.7	2,782.4	2.4
Not Offering Shares	567.3	0.8	216.7	0.2
Investment Objective				
Aggressive Growth	$ 5,299.9	7.9%	$ 7,210.9	6.2%
Growth	8,030.3	12.0	10,915.8	9.4
Growth & Income	7,710.6	11.5	10,961.1	9.4
Precious Metals	683.4	1.0	1,839.2	1.6
International	1,746.0	2.6	3,040.6	2.6
Global Equity	1,212.0	1.8	2,003.0	1.7
Flexible Portfolio	177.8	0.3	488.9	0.4
Balanced	514.6	0.8	1,112.2	1.0
Income-Equity	1,389.3	2.1	2,734.8	2.4
Income-Mixed	3,381.7	5.0	4,811.5	4.1
Income-Bond	1,642.6	2.5	3,189.6	2.7
Option/Income	1,105.4	1.6	1,472.4	1.3
U.S. Government Income	14,060.0	21.0	27,406.4	23.6
Ginnie Mae	6,975.0	10.4	12,994.0	11.2
Global Bond	27.8	0.0	488.8	0.4
Corporate Bond	871.3	1.3	2,233.4	1.9
High-Yield Bond	3,127.9	4.7	5,899.7	5.1
Long-Term Municipal Bond	6,381.0	9.5	11,688.9	10.1
Long-Term State Municipal Bond	2,676.1	4.0	5,733.1	4.9

Redemptions of Mutual Funds by Investment Objective Within Method of Sales

1984–1987

(Millions of Dollars)

Sales Force

	1984	1985	1986	1987
Aggressive Growth	$ 922.9	$ 1,488.8	$ 1,736.0	$ 2,621.8
Growth	2,516.2	3,796.8	4,834.0	6,037.9
Growth & Income	1,676.8	2,452.5	4,680.8	6,211.9
Precious Metals	16.2	159.9	230.6	562.7
International	48.2	72.0	425.7	1,203.2
Global Equity	413.7	766.9	1,181.2	1,965.4
Flexible Portfolio	69.1	85.5	149.4	417.0
Balanced	208.4	197.7	360.6	777.1
Income-Equity	327.9	277.9	798.5	1,701.4
Income-Mixed	1,122.4	1,552.7	2,691.7	4,093.9
Income-Bond	309.3	343.4	1,028.2	2,083.5
Option/Income	248.6	603.8	1,074.2	1,271.4
U.S. Government Income	748.7	4,653.9	13,308.3	26,124.7
Ginnie Mae	389.3	1,527.4	6,041.1	10,545.0
Global Bond	5.1	6.6	27.2	420.5
Corporate Bond	311.6	387.5	763.3	1,756.6
High-Yield Bond	753.0	938.1	2,190.7	3,995.1
Long-Term Municipal Bond	2,138.8	1,277.3	2,980.3	6,189.1
Long-Term State Municipal Bond	348.9	535.6	1,426.1	3,550.2
Total	**$ 12,575.1**	**$ 21,124.3**	**$45,927.9**	**$81,528.4**

Direct Marketing

	1984	1985	1986	1987
Aggressive Growth	$ 1,901.6	$ 3,371.3	$ 3,441.6	$ 4,252.2
Growth	1,111.2	1,735.8	2,664.4	3,919.3
Growth & Income	919.2	1,592.3	2,525.4	4,149.2
Precious Metals	61.3	321.6	452.7	1,275.8
International	112.6	260.5	1,320.3	1,836.7
Global Equity	0.0	0.0	0.7	21.3
Flexible Portfolio	2.9	14.5	19.1	47.4
Balanced	80.1	80.0	153.2	325.9
Income-Equity	164.8	221.3	590.8	1,033.3
Income-Mixed	230.5	301.1	503.4	684.4
Income-Bond	278.1	315.6	577.2	936.5
Option/Income	24.3	54.3	29.1	199.8
U.S. Government Income	63.1	146.3	731.1	1,117.8
Ginnie Mae	38.6	97.4	875.6	2,284.2
Global Bond	0.0	0.0	0.6	68.3
Corporate Bond	36.1	35.7	69.7	286.8
High-Yield Bond	63.4	188.9	803.1	1,575.2
Long-Term Municipal Bond	1,602.2	2,035.3	3,400.7	5,499.7
Long-Term State Municipal Bond	167.9	449.7	1,249.9	2,183.0
Total	**$ 6,857.9**	**$ 11,221.6**	**$ 19,408.6**	**$ 31,696.8**

Sales of Equity, Bond, and Income Fund Shares
by State and Geographical Regions
Within Method of Sales
1987
(Thousands of Dollars)

	Sales Force	Direct Marketing	Total
New England	**$ 9,378,453**	**$ 6,885,118**	**$16,263,571**
Connecticut	2,789,216	1,072,948	3,862,164
Maine	411,046	173,144	584,190
Massachusetts	4,839,971	5,120,225	9,960,196
New Hampshire	582,264	229,191	811,455
Rhode Island	487,463	204,024	691,487
Vermont	268,493	85,586	354,079
Middle Atlantic	**$25,102,268**	**$11,213,829**	**$36,316,097**
New Jersey	6,401,167	2,175,055	8,576,222
New York	11,646,709	7,055,920	18,702,629
Pennsylvania	7,054,392	1,982,854	9,037,246
East North Central	**$22,442,956**	**$ 7,420,504**	**$29,863,460**
Illinois	6,533,953	2,688,358	9,222,311
Indiana	2,318,850	580,539	2,899,389
Michigan	5,028,383	1,320,701	6,349,084
Ohio	5,785,513	2,126,413	7,911,926
Wisconsin	2,776,257	704,493	3,480,750
West North Central	**$12,463,498**	**$ 2,494,115**	**$14,957,613**
Iowa	1,822,133	213,410	2,035,543
Kansas	1,331,810	303,812	1,635,622
Minnesota	3,331,307	819,949	4,151,256
Missouri	3,762,121	825,451	4,587,572
Nebraska	1,202,561	201,696	1,404,257
North Dakota	533,159	83,214	616,373
South Dakota	480,407	46,583	526,990
South Atlantic	**$19,178,726**	**$ 7,981,407**	**$27,160,133**
Delaware	396,712	137,062	533,774
District of Columbia	578,473	267,963	846,436
Florida	7,904,649	2,667,173	10,571,822
Georgia	1,944,450	887,636	2,832,086
Maryland	2,285,869	1,620,406	3,906,275
North Carolina	2,424,938	885,186	3,310,124
South Carolina	800,653	250,645	1,051,298
Virginia	2,328,937	1,178,890	3,507,827
West Virginia	514,045	86,446	600,491

Sales of Equity, Bond, and Income Fund Shares
by State and Geographical Regions
Within Method of Sales
1987
(Thousands of Dollars)

	Sales Force	Direct Marketing	Total
East South Central	$ 5,205,473	$ 1,073,605	$ 6,279,078
Alabama	1,462,115	245,076	1,707,191
Kentucky	1,084,903	258,676	1,343,579
Mississippi	665,664	129,055	794,719
Tennessee	1,992,791	440,798	2,433,589
West South Central	$ 11,063,319	$ 3,613,234	$ 14,676,553
Arkansas	1,134,250	182,229	1,316,479
Louisiana	1,782,849	339,805	2,122,654
Oklahoma	1,388,759	275,437	1,664,196
Texas	6,757,461	2,815,763	9,573,224
Mountain	$ 7,778,225	$ 2,163,846	$ 9,942,071
Arizona	2,407,268	617,534	3,024,802
Colorado	2,639,779	782,173	3,421,952
Idaho	419,298	88,118	507,416
Montana	461,985	57,993	519,978
Nevada	485,334	172,497	657,831
New Mexico	528,998	242,312	771,310
Utah	593,723	160,583	754,306
Wyoming	241,840	42,636	284,476
Pacific	$ 18,486,989	$ 9,733,593	$ 28,220,582
Alaska	248,612	70,144	318,756
California	13,589,727	8,007,099	21,596,826
Hawaii	452,203	193,674	645,877
Oregon	1,527,465	451,997	1,979,462
Washington	2,668,982	1,010,679	3,679,661
U.S. Territories & Possessions	$ 276,339	$ 48,738	$ 325,077
Canada	$ 81,943	$ 70,834	$ 152,777
Other Countries	$ 556,944	$ 368,614	$ 925,558
Total	$132,015,133	$53,067,437	$185,082,570

Sales of Equity, Bond, and Income Fund Shares
by State and Geographical Regions
Within Method of Sales
1987
(Percent of Total)

	Sales Force	Direct Marketing	Total
New England	**7.11%**	**12.97%**	**8.79%**
Connecticut	2.11	2.02	2.09
Maine	0.31	0.33	0.32
Massachusetts	3.68	9.65	5.38
New Hampshire	0.44	0.43	0.44
Rhode Island	0.37	0.38	0.37
Vermont	0.20	0.16	0.19
Middle Atlantic	**19.01%**	**21.13%**	**19.62%**
New Jersey	4.85	4.10	4.63
New York	8.82	13.29	10.11
Pennsylvania	5.34	3.74	4.88
East North Central	**17.00%**	**13.98%**	**16.14%**
Illinois	4.95	5.07	4.98
Indiana	1.76	1.09	1.58
Michigan	3.81	2.49	3.43
Ohio	4.38	4.00	4.27
Wisconsin	2.10	1.33	1.88
West North Central	**9.44%**	**4.70%**	**8.08%**
Iowa	1.38	0.40	1.10
Kansas	1.01	0.57	0.88
Minnesota	2.52	1.54	2.24
Missouri	2.86	1.56	2.48
Nebraska	0.91	0.38	0.76
North Dakota	0.40	0.16	0.33
South Dakota	0.36	.09	0.29
South Atlantic	**14.53%**	**15.04%**	**14.67%**
Delaware	0.30	0.26	0.29
District of Columbia	0.44	0.51	0.46
Florida	5.99	5.03	5.71
Georgia	1.47	1.67	1.53
Maryland	1.73	3.05	2.11
North Carolina	1.84	1.67	1.79
South Carolina	0.61	0.47	0.57
Virginia	1.76	2.22	1.89
West Virginia	0.39	0.16	0.32

Sales of Equity, Bond, and Income Fund Shares
by State and Geographical Regions
Within Method of Sales
1987
(Percent of Total)

	Sales Force	Direct Marketing	Total
East South Central	**3.94%**	**2.02%**	**3.39%**
Alabama	1.11	0.46	0.92
Kentucky	0.82	0.49	0.73
Mississippi	0.50	0.24	0.43
Tennessee	1.51	0.83	1.31
West South Central	**8.38%**	**6.81%**	**7.93%**
Arkansas	0.86	0.34	0.71
Louisiana	1.35	0.64	1.15
Oklahoma	1.05	0.52	0.90
Texas	5.12	5.31	5.17
Mountain	**5.89%**	**4.08%**	**5.37%**
Arizona	1.82	1.16	1.63
Colorado	2.00	1.47	1.85
Idaho	0.32	0.17	0.27
Montana	0.35	0.11	0.28
Nevada	0.37	0.33	0.36
New Mexico	0.40	0.46	0.42
Utah	0.45	0.30	0.41
Wyoming	0.18	0.08	0.15
Pacific	**14.01%**	**18.34%**	**15.25%**
Alaska	0.19	0.13	0.17
California	10.30	15.09	11.67
Hawaii	0.34	0.37	0.35
Oregon	1.16	0.85	1.07
Washington	2.02	1.90	1.99
U.S. Territories & Possessions	**0.21%**	**0.10%**	**0.18%**
Canada	**0.06%**	**0.13%**	**0.08%**
Other	**0.42%**	**0.70%**	**0.50%**
Total	**100.00%**	**100.00%**	**100.00%**

Total Purchases, Total Sales, and Net Purchases of Portfolio Securities by Mutual Funds
1970–1987
(Millions of Dollars)

Year	Total Purchases	Total Sales	Net Purchases
1970	$ 20,405.0	$ 18,588.5	$ 1,816.5
1971	25,360.2	24,793.8	566.4
1972	24,467.6	25,823.6	(1,356.0)
1973	19,706.6	21,903.0	(2,196.4)
1974	12,299.7	12,213.5	86.2
1975	15,396.9	15,511.4	(114.5)
1976	15,348.2	16,881.2	(1,533.0)
1977	18,168.0	19,420.7	(1,252.7)
1978	20,945.6	23,069.7	(2,124.1)
1979	22,412.1	23,702.5	(1,290.4)
1980	32,987.2	32,080.6	906.6
1981	36,161.7	33,709.2	2,452.5
1982	55,682.0	47,920.7	7,761.3
1983	93,009.5	71,466.5	21,543.0
1984	119,272.4	98,929.6	20,342.8
1985	259,578.5	186,974.6	72,603.9
1986	501,058.5	365,167.6	135,890.9
1987	531,075.8	485,640.1	45,435.7

NOTE: Parentheses indicate net portfolio sales.

Total Purchases, Total Sales, and Net Purchases of Common Stocks by Mutual Funds

1970–1987

(Millions of Dollars)

Year	Total Purchases	Total Sales	Net Purchases
1970	$ 17,127.6	$ 15,900.8	$ 1,226.8
1971	21,557.7	21,175.1	382.6
1972	20,943.5	22,552.8	(1,609.3)
1973	15,560.7	17,504.4	(1,943.7)
1974	9,085.3	9,372.1	(286.8)
1975	10,948.7	11,902.3	(953.6)
1976	10,729.1	13,278.3	(2,549.2)
1977	8,704.7	12,211.3	(3,506.6)
1978	12,832.9	14,454.7	(1,621.8)
1979	13,089.0	15,923.0	(2,834.0)
1980	19,893.8	21,799.9	(1,906.1)
1981	20,859.7	21,278.3	(418.6)
1982	27,397.2	24,939.6	2,457.6
1983	54,581.7	40,813.9	13,767.8
1984	56,587.9	50,895.0	5,692.9
1985	80,783.1	72,577.3	8,205.8
1986	134,711.0	118,091.9	16,619.1
1987	199,042.0	176,084.9	22,957.1

NOTE: Parentheses indicate net portfolio sales.

Total Purchases, Total Sales, and Net Purchases of Securities Other Than Common Stocks by Mutual Funds

1970–1987

(Millions of Dollars)

Year	Total Purchases	Total Sales	Net Purchases
1970	$ 3,277.4	$ 2,687.7	$ 589.7
1971	3,802.5	3,618.6	183.9
1972	3,524.1	3,270.9	253.2
1973	4,145.9	4,398.7	(252.8)
1974	3,214.4	2,841.4	373.0
1975	4,448.2	3,609.1	839.1
1976	4,619.1	3,602.9	1,016.2
1977	9,463.3	7,209.4	2,253.9
1978	8,112.7	8,615.0	(502.3)
1979	9,323.1	7,779.5	1,543.6
1980	13,093.4	10,280.7	2,812.7
1981	15,302.0	12,430.9	2,871.1
1982	28,284.8	22,981.1	5,303.7
1983	38,427.7	30,652.6	7,775.1
1984	62,684.6	48,034.6	14,650.0
1985	178,795.3	114,397.3	64,398.0
1986	366,347.5	247,075.7	119,271.8
1987	332,033.8	309,555.2	22,478.6

NOTE: Parentheses indicate net portfolio sales.

Portfolio Purchases and Sales by Fund Characteristics

(Millions of Dollars)

	1986		1987	
	Purchases	**Sales**	**Purchases**	**Sales**
All Securities	**$501,058.5**	**$365,167.6**	**$531,075.8**	**$485,640.1**
Method of Sales				
Sales Force	$ 387,193.0R	$ 280,001.8R	$ 380,253.3	$ 343,174.2
Direct Marketing	105,171.9R	79,373.6R	135,227.8	129,308.6
Not Offering Shares	275.7	421.5	276.0	341.9
Variable Annuities	8,417.9	5,370.7	15,318.7	12,815.4
Investment Objective				
Aggressive Growth	$ 27,547.4	$ 25,738.8	$ 43,000.0	$ 40,908.8
Growth	37,430.3	36,584.8	53,996.4	49,757.3
Growth & Income	41,300.8	32,427.2	62,631.5	50,891.6
Precious Metals	777.6	701.5	3,075.8	1,731.2
International	6,627.3	4,259.5	8,901.9	11,386.7
Global Equity	5,128.6	3,886.7	6,751.4	5,706.6
Flexible Portfolio	1,266.4	970.7	9,841.8	7,629.1
Balanced	8,318.7	5,811.6	11,365.6	9,836.9
Income-Equity	11,006.2	7,702.6	18,708.2	15,124.6
Income-Mixed	10,494.5	7,074.5	13,450.6	12,681.7
Income-Bond	15,267.2	11,870.2	13,964.5	12,451.6
Option/Income	14,977.7	14,154.2	13,938.9	14,140.8
U.S. Government Income	163,527.8	123,097.1	133,289.2	120,969.3
Ginnie Mae	52,723.9	29,700.3	41,718.0	41,804.8
Global Bond	851.6	547.6	3,571.6	2,247.8
Corporate Bond	10,845.4	7,367.2	10,029.2	9,105.6
High-Yield Bond	29,615.5	19,131.2	25,397.9	24,209.6
Long-Term Municipal Bond	44,865.8	28,029.6	40,932.6	40,525.5
Long-Term State Municipal Bond	18,485.8	6,112.3	16,510.7	14,530.6

R—Revised

	1986		1987	
	Purchases	**Sales**	**Purchases**	**Sales**
Common Stock Only	**$134,711.0**	**$118,091.9**	**$199,042.0**	**$176,084.9**
Method of Sales				
Sales Force	$ 80,304.0R	$ 72,396.0R	$113,529.4	$ 98,997.6
Direct Marketing	50,313.6R	42,736.3R	77,494.8	70,807.7
Not Offering Shares	268.7	409.3	254.9	337.8
Variable Annuities	3,824.7	2,550.3	7,762.9	5,941.8
Investment Objective				
Aggressive Growth	$ 26,648.0	$ 24,929.6	$ 40,873.7	$ 38,563.5
Growth	35,724.3	34,885.7	51,865.3	48,051.2
Growth & Income	29,010.5	23,695.9	46,677.2	36,008.0
Precious Metals	726.9	648.4	2,933.4	1,634.1
International	6,202.0	3,899.4	8,249.7	10,909.3
Global Equity	4,540.8	3,407.6	6,366.4	5,362.1
Flexible Portfolio	756.8	645.3	4,499.6	2,833.2
Balanced	3,574.6	2,316.4	4,768.1	3,594.4
Income-Equity	7,192.4	5,111.9	13,751.4	10,238.5
Income-Mixed	3,072.7	2,727.8	3,556.4	3,573.0
Income-Bond	943.1	871.9	588.3	510.9
Option/Income	14,711.6	13,761.6	13,625.0	14,007.9
U.S. Government Income	0.8	1.4	124.8	34.7
Ginnie Mae	164.1	45.3	0.0	0.0
Global Bond	18.6	0.0	301.2	110.6
Corporate Bond	125.4	63.5	195.3	42.0
High-Yield Bond	1,297.5	1,079.7	663.8	611.5
Long-Term Municipal Bond	0.6	0.5	0.0	0.0
Long-Term State Municipal Bond	0.3	0.0	2.4	0.0

R—Revised

Total Short-Term Funds*
1980–1987
(Millions of Dollars)

Yearend	Total Sales	Total Redemptions	Net Sales	Number of Funds	Total Accounts Outstanding	Total Net Assets
1980	$ 237,427.7	$ 207,877.7	$ 29,550.0	106	4,762,103	$ 76,361.3
1981	462,422.6	354,972.1	107,450.5	179	10,323,466	186,158.2
1982	611,202.9	580,778.4	30,424.5	318	13,258,143	219,837.5
1983	507,447.0	551,151.3	(43,704.3)	373	12,539,688	179,386.5
1984	634,226.7	586,992.4	47,234.3	427	13,844,697	233,553.8
1985	839,498.8	831,121.2	8,377.6	460	14,954,726	243,802.4
1986	989,816.0	948,641.3	41,174.7	487	16,313,148	292,151.6
1987	1,060,947.6	1,062,526.8	(1,579.2)	543	17,674,790	316,096.1

* Figures are totals for money market and short-term municipal bond funds.

Comparable data for long-term funds can be found on page 65, 70.

An Overview: Money Market Funds*
1974–1987

(Millions of Dollars)

Year End	Total Sales	Total Redemptions	Net Sales	Number of Funds	Total Accounts Outstanding	Average Maturity (Days)	Total Net Assets
1974	$ 2,232.0	$ 556.0	$ 1,676.0	15	n.a.	n.a.	$ 1,715.1
1975	6,748.7	5,883.9	864.8	36	208,777	93	3,695.7
1976	9,360.9	9,609.2	(248.3)	48	180,676	110	3,685.8
1977	10,673.0	10,662.7	10.3	50	177,522	76	3,887.7
1978	30,452.2	24,294.5	6,157.7	61	467,803	42	10,858.0
1979	111,855.1	78,363.4	33,491.7	76	2,307,852	34	45,214.2
1980	232,172.8	204,068.5	28,104.3	96	4,745,572	24	74,447.7
1981	451,889.5	346,701.5	105,188.0	159	10,282,095	34	181,910.4
1982	581,758.9	559,581.1	22,177.8	281	13,101,347	37	206,607.5
1983	462,978.7	508,729.9	(45,751.2)	307	12,276,639	37	162,549.5
1984	571,959.3	531,050.9	40,908.4	329	13,556,180	43	209,731.9
1985	730,073.8	732,343.0	(2,269.2)	348	14,435,386	37	207,535.3
1986	792,349.1	776,303.2	16,045.9	360	15,653,595	40	228,345.8
1987	869,097.6	865,675.5	3,422.1	389	16,832,666	31	254,676.4

* A small percentage of funds report assets and liquid assets but not sales and redemptions. In the interest of comparability, these latter two sets of figures have been adjusted upward.

An Overview: Short-Term Municipal Bond Funds
1980–1987

(Millions of Dollars)

Yearend	Total Sales	Total Redemptions	Net Sales	Number of Funds	Total Accounts Outstanding	Total Net Assets
1980	$ 5,254.9	$ 3,809.2	$ 1,445.7	10	16,531	$ 1,913.6
1981	10,533.1	8,270.6	2,262.5	20	41,371	4,247.8
1982	29,444.0	21,197.3	8,246.7	37	156,796	13,230.0
1983	44,468.3	42,421.4	2,046.9	66	263,049	16,837.0
1984	62,267.4	55,941.5	6,325.9	97	288,517	23,821.9
1985	109,425.0	98,778.2	10,646.8	112	499,245	36,267.1
1986						
National	188,017.3	165,329.1	22,688.2	101	604,055	59,367.5
State	9,449.7	7,009.1	2,440.6	26	55,498	4,438.2
1987						
National	179,215.0	185,031.1	(5,816.1)	112	731,265	54,555.8
State	12,635.1	11,820.2	814.9	42	110,859	6,863.9

Money Market Fund Monthly Assets

(Thousands of Dollars)

	Total	General Purpose	Broker/Dealer	Institutional
1985				
January	$214,506,601	$63,877,061	$ 95,141,818	$55,487,722
February	210,284,846	63,733,357	95,350,490	51,200,999
March	206,708,367	63,742,342	94,461,725	48,504,300
April	207,795,769	62,352,639	93,061,345	52,381,785
May	212,600,984	61,990,649	93,708,519	56,901,816
June	211,815,456	61,363,895	94,200,660	56,250,901
July	208,827,389	60,863,364	94,721,370	53,242,655
August	208,356,239	61,288,697	94,289,570	52,777,972
September	206,524,421	61,554,870	93,416,808	51,552,743
October	208,318,271	61,061,464	93,524,551	53,732,256
November	208,107,794	60,623,118	93,609,462	53,875,214
December	207,535,297	60,178,849	93,199,396	54,157,052
1986				
January	$210,615,429	$60,287,636	$ 95,685,132	$54,642,661
February	208,560,133	58,891,053	96,135,696	53,533,384
March	212,287,124	59,152,306	98,858,947	56,275,871
April	221,947,239	59,628,242	100,841,607	61,477,390
May	223,909,672	61,200,777	101,558,046	61,150,849
June	222,012,597	61,642,027	101,231,483	59,139,087
July	229,509,853	62,880,871	102,817,552	63,811,430
August	231,585,019	62,074,260	102,190,551	67,320,208
September	234,465,394	65,294,526	104,120,377	65,050,491
October	233,670,749	64,043,419	103,961,125	65,666,205
November	232,439,051	63,485,188	104,012,724	64,941,139
December	228,345,828	63,316,578	103,298,324	61,730,926
1987				
January	$232,478,532	$60,988,081	$106,398,732	$65,091,719
February	235,595,971	62,143,193	107,774,640	65,678,138
March	234,242,627	62,075,713	107,399,569	64,767,345
April	235,429,006	66,054,314	105,307,665	64,067,027
May	237,529,767	67,917,069	105,168,355	64,444,343
June	234,783,689	66,801,688	103,587,638	64,394,363
July	239,192,670	67,448,174	105,342,003	66,402,493
August	242,579,672	69,555,153	106,868,707	66,155,812
September	241,255,386	71,269,312	106,487,402	63,498,672
October	254,850,878	78,363,282	106,727,188	69,760,408
November	259,685,594	78,194,792	108,015,274	73,475,528
December	254,676,440	78,321,502	106,682,635	69,672,303

Money Market Funds Asset Composition
Money Market Yearend, 1982–1987

(Millions of Dollars)

	1982	1983	1984	1985	1986	1987
Total Net Assets	$206,607.5	$162,549.5	$209,731.9R	$207,535.3	$228,345.8	$254,676.4
U.S. Treasury Bills	37,935.9	20,484.0	20,197.9	20,391.5	20,428.6	4,944.0
Other Treasury Securities	4,706.0	2,354.6	5,214.7	4,271.9	7,602.9	9,358.6
Other U.S. Securities	11,972.0	13,375.2	16,974.3	18,043.1	15,120.3	26,998.9
Repurchase Agreements	16,222.1	13,028.5	22,769.8	26,068.6	32,160.1	39,290.6
Commercial Bank CDs(1)	35,479.4	18,931.3	18,362.5	13,256.3	13,427.2	24,216.9
Other Domestic CDs(2)	5,310.9	5,107.4	5,270.7	3,578.5	5,684.3	9,333.7
Eurodollar CDs(3)	23,758.8	21,911.1	21,213.5	19,027.0	22,168.4	21,611.7
Commercial Paper	50,327.1	46,752.6	78,408.1	87,555.4	94,882.0	100,534.4
Bankers' Acceptances	18,776.1	19,586.2	19,564.2	11,578.3	10,405.7	10,771.2
Cash Reserves	278.3	(274.5)	(1,244.5)	154.8	(24.9)	(326.7)
Other	1,840.9	1,293.1	3,000.7	3,609.9	6,491.2	7,943.1
Average Maturity(4)	37	37	43	37	40	31
Number of Funds	281	307	329	348	360	389

(1) Commercial bank CDs are those issued by American banks located in the U.S.
(2) Other Domestic CDs include those issued by S&Ls and American branches of foreign banks.
(3) Eurodollar CDs are those issued by foreign branches of domestic banks and some issued by Canadian banks; this category includes some one day paper.
(4) Maturity of each individual security in the portfolio at end of month weighted by its value.

Comparable data for long-term funds can be found on pages 82–85.

Money Market Fund
Shareholder Accounts by Type of Fund

	General Purpose	Broker/ Dealer	Institutional	Total
1985				
January	5,021,181	8,523,450	123,833	13,668,464
February	5,023,699	8,632,625	124,895	13,781,219
March	4,992,789	8,752,744	116,437	13,861,970
April	5,011,501	9,135,643	122,548	14,269,692
May	4,951,336	9,197,504	113,499	14,262,339
June	4,919,843	9,244,749	114,216	14,278,808
July	4,896,480	9,394,805	119,468	14,410,753
August	4,898,130	9,435,718	134,816	14,468,664
September	4,883,179	9,434,034	144,597	14,461,810
October	4,861,777	9,464,960	148,340	14,475,077
November	4,825,014	9,450,008	141,579	14,416,601
December	4,795,441	9,503,382	136,563	14,435,386
1986				
January	4,755,720	9,593,273	137,829	14,486,822
February	4,815,685	9,701,239	134,022	14,650,946
March	4,912,296	9,902,169	137,049	14,951,514
April	4,967,756	10,345,979	141,512	15,455,247
May	4,958,173	10,336,859	145,785	15,440,817
June	4,965,974	10,380,050	144,306	15,490,330
July	4,963,533	10,471,572	143,511	15,578,616
August	4,937,707	10,483,803	143,362	15,564,872
September	4,993,508	10,554,627	144,976	15,693,111
October	4,982,390	10,572,966	136,604	15,691,960
November	4,932,956	10,579,632	134,509	15,647,097
December	4,889,141	10,623,590	140,864	15,653,595
1987				
January	4,797,360	10,723,207	143,019	15,663,586
February	4,799,661	10,763,009	141,378	15,704,048
March	4,788,670	10,912,577	138,327	15,839,574
April	4,947,334	11,208,138	140,922	16,296,394
May	4,979,964	11,288,344	142,921	16,411,229
June	4,962,648	11,181,233	144,033	16,287,914
July	4,981,636	11,213,898	128,857	16,324,391
August	4,986,780	11,294,936	124,558	16,406,274
September	5,039,203	11,541,156	125,241	16,705,600
October	5,227,676	11,437,447	141,938	16,807,061
November	5,259,616	11,361,473	139,240	16,760,329
December	5,266,231	11,422,519	143,916	16,832,666

Sales Due to Exchanges by Investment Objective
1986–1987
(Millions of Dollars)

Investment Objective	1986	1987
Aggressive Growth	$12,106.4	$28,267.5
Growth	6,390.8	10,369.5
Growth & Income	12,097.0	19,962.7
Precious Metals	1,522.3	8,745.5
International	3,314.0	3,872.7
Global Equity	305.0	561.3
Flexible Portfolio	46.8	385.7
Balanced	264.2	741.0
Income-Equity	1,488.2	2,722.0
Income-Mixed	790.2	1,173.5
Income-Bond	1,196.7	1,898.0
Option/Income	155.8	288.5
U.S. Government Income	2,062.8	4,013.3
Ginnie. Mae	2,033.0	1,988.2
Global Bond	37.3	437.9
Corporate Bond	1,191.5	1,595.4
High-Yield Bond	2,791.7	3,397.7
Long-Term Municipal Bond	9,079.0	12,569.0
Long-Term State Municipal Bond	2,241.9	3,903.2
Short-Term National Municipal Bond	6,836.1	15,420.1
Short-Term State Municipal Bond	959.0	3,175.5
Money Market	40,908.7	83,423.6

Redemptions Due to Exchanges
by Investment Objective
1986–1987
(Millions of Dollars)

Investment Objective	1986	1987
Aggressive Growth	$14,842.6	$30,544.0
Growth	8,037.1	11,610.4
Growth & Income	12,317.0	20,889.4
Precious Metals	1,460.5	8,423.6
International	3,233.3	6,039.5
Global Equity	303.3	747.8
Flexible Portfolio	39.6	189.5
Balanced	223.5	958.2
Income-Equity	1,367.3	3,499.9
Income-Mixed	714.3	1,605.0
Income-Bond	1,006.1	2,182.1
Option/Income	465.6	715.5
U.S. Government Income	2,121.4	8,908.6
Ginnie Mae	2,465.4	4,806.3
Global Bond	12.7	348.6
Corporate Bond	918.0	1,978.6
High-Yield Bond	2,690.8	5,172.7
Long-Term Municipal Bond	9,294.0	17,485.9
Long-Term State Municipal Bond	1,963.9	6,214.5
Short-Term National Municipal Bond	5,857.1	9,737.0
Short-Term State Municipal Bond	734.1	1,765.6
Money Market	37,945.2	63,633.4

Net Sales Due to Exchanges by Investment Objective
1986–1987
(Millions of Dollars)

Investment Objective	1986	1987
Aggressive Growth	$(2,736.2)	$(2,276.5)
Growth	(1,646.3)	(1,240.9)
Growth & Income	(220.0)	(926.7)
Precious Metals	61.8	321.9
International	80.7	(2,166.8)
Global Equity	1.7	(186.5)
Flexible Portfolio	7.2	196.2
Balanced	40.7	(217.2)
Income-Equity	120.9	(777.9)
Income-Mixed	75.9	(431.5)
Income-Bond	190.6	(284.1)
Option/Income	(309.8)	(427.0)
U.S. Government Income	(58.6)	(4,895.3)
Ginnie Mae	(432.4)	(2,818.1)
Global Bond	24.6	89.3
Corporate Bond	273.5	(383.2)
High-Yield Bond	100.9	(1,775.0)
Long-Term Municipal Bond	(215.0)	(4,916.9)
Long-Term State Municipal Bond	278.0	(2,311.3)
Short-Term National Municipal Bond	979.0	5,683.1
Short-Term State Municipal Bond	224.9	1,409.9
Money Market	2,963.5	19,790.2

IRA Assets and Accounts by Investment Objective Yearend 1987

Investment Objective	Assets		Accounts	
	Millions of Dollars	Percent	Number (Thousands)	Percent
Aggressive Growth	$7,528.3	10.4%	1,886.4	12.6%
Growth	7,645.9	10.6	1,773.4	11.9
Growth & Income	10,821.9	15.0	2,236.6	14.9
Precious Metals	823.4	1.1	248.5	1.7
International	1,117.5	1.5	316.3	2.1
Global Equity	2,176.1	3.0	463.1	3.1
Flexible Portfolio	235.3	0.3	56.5	0.4
Balanced	999.9	1.4	214.6	1.4
Income-Equity	3,528.9	4.9	779.4	5.2
Income-Mixed	1,176.3	1.6	203.3	1.3
Income-Bond	1,646.8	2.3	225.9	1.5
Option/Income	764.6	1.1	158.1	1.1
U.S. Government Income	10,307.2	14.2	1,289.7	8.6
Ginnie Mae	4,175.8	5.8	632.6	4.2
Global Bond	117.6	0.2	11.3	0.1
Corporate Bond	1,529.2	2.1	192.0	1.3
High-Yield Bond	4,234.7	5.9	609.9	4.1
Money Market	13,415.9	18.6	3,660.3	24.5
Total	**$72,245.3**	**100.0%**	**14,957.9**	**100.0%**

Self-Employed Retirement Plan Assets and Accounts by Investment Objective Yearend 1987

Investment Objective	Assets		Accounts	
	Millions of Dollars	Percent	Number (Thousands)	Percent
Aggressive Growth	$ 953.9	9.5%	87.8	10.3%
Growth	1,501.0	14.9	76.2	8.9
Growth & Income	1,697.4	16.8	78.8	9.3
Precious Metals	119.2	1.2	12.5	1.5
International	112.2	1.1	11.6	1.4
Global Equity	168.3	1.7	9.0	1.0
Flexible Portfolio	42.1	0.4	7.6	0.9
Balanced	91.2	0.9	7.7	0.9
Income-Equity	343.7	3.4	28.2	3.3
Income-Mixed	182.4	1.8	10.8	1.3
Income-Bond	350.7	3.5	19.7	2.3
Option/Income	35.1	0.3	2.2	0.3
U.S. Government Income	339.7	3.3	26.5	3.1
Ginnie Mae	413.8	4.1	32.3	3.8
Global Bond	14.0	0.1	0.9	0.1
Corporate Bond	273.6	2.7	13.9	1.6
High-Yield Bond	378.8	3.8	22.4	2.6
Money Market	3,080.4	30.5	404.4	47.4
Total	**$10,097.5**	**100.0%**	**852.5**	**100.0%**

An Overview: Fiduciary, Business, and Institutional Investors in Equity, Bond, and Income Funds

Year	Reporting Companies' Assets (In Millions)	Percent Assets of Total Members' Assets	Reported Institutional Accounts In Force	Reported Value of Holdings (In Millions)	Reported Institutional Holdings as a Percent of Total Net Assets
1970	$ 32,631.1	68.5%	1,071,243	$ 6,174.0	18.9%
1972	44,696.4	74.7	1,119,243	8,906.9	19.9
1974	26,981.4	75.4	1,440,533	7,116.1	26.4
1976	39,342.2	77.3	1,346,490	10,719.7	27.2
1978	37,043.3	82.4	1,258,996	9,590.5	25.9
1980	45,763.2	78.4	1,023,101	12,855.9	28.1
1981	48,364.0	87.6	771,585	11,405.3	23.6
1982	66,569.2	86.7	953,483	16,232.7	24.4
1983	99,911.0	88.0	1,327,304	23,314.8	23.8
1984	126,354.1	92.1	1,415,021	30,304.3	24.0
1985	213,821.7	85.0	2,066,265	52,697.9	24.6
1986	359,355.4	84.7	4,072,491	102,063.3	28.4
1987*	337,958.1	74.5	3,665,001	89,549.0	26.5

NOTE: Prior to 1981, Keogh and IRA figures are included in institutional holdings. Institutional holdings as a percent of assets of reporting companies are slightly understated prior to 1974 due to limited reporting of Keogh information. Reported institutional accounts and value of holdings for 1981 and 1982 were used to derive universe estimates shown in the following tables which present institutional data in greater detail. The 1981 figures were revised to exclude Keogh and IRA. In the 1980 figures, Keogh and IRA accounted for about 30 percent of institutional accounts and 23 percent of institutional assets.

*Preliminary

Number of Accounts of Fiduciary, Business, and Institutional Investors in Equity, Bond, and Income Funds

	1984R	1985	1986	1987*
Fiduciaries (Banks and Individuals Serving as Trustees, Guardians, and Administrators)	**951,221**	**1,300,822**	**2,551,502R**	**2,753,993**
Business Corporations	72,401	111,481	169,878	168,034
Retirement Plans	428,089	926,880	1,301,371R	1,703,425
Insurance Companies and Other Financial Institutions	13,743	21,045	50,234	88,730
Unions	1,718	770	1,590	3,284
Total Business Organizations	**515,951**	**1,060,176**	**1,523,073R**	**1,963,473**
Churches and Religious Organizations	9,007	11,108	16,607	19,814
Fraternal, Welfare, and Other Public Associations	6,627	7,801	13,949	11,663
Hospitals, Sanitariums, Orphanages, Etc.	3,075	2,566	7,019	5,500
Schools and Colleges	4,286	4,415	6,055	6,457
Foundations	1,090	4,657	5,213R	7,660
Total Institutions and Foundations	**24,085**	**30,547**	**48,843R**	**51,094**
Other Institutional Investors Not Classified (a)	**87,700**	**65,887**	**209,315**	**246,046**
Total	**1,587,957**	**2,457,432**	**4,332,733R**	**5,014,606**

(a) Includes institutional accounts which do not fall under other classifications and those for which no determination of classification can be made.

NOTE: Reporters of institutional data represented 92.1% of total shareholder accounts in 1984, 83.3% in 1985, 82.6% in 1986, and 71.4% in 1987. The figures shown above are universe-estimated based on those reports.

R—Revised

*Preliminary

Number of Accounts of Fiduciary, Business, and Institutional Investors in Money Market Funds

	1984R	1985	1986	1987*
Fiduciaries (Banks and Individuals Serving as Trustees, Guardians, and Administrators)	**614,990**	**747,968**	**799,847**	**1,356,332**
Business Corporations	299,793	245,211	273,416	264,159
Retirement Plans	299,823	378,893	374,303	432,862
Insurance Companies and Other Financial Institutions	52,373	19,530	25,613	24,406
Unions	1,053	953	3,843	10,049
Total Business Organizations	**653,042**	**644,587**	**677,175**	**731,476**
Churches and Religious Organizations	19,435	15,746	15,165	15,989
Fraternal, Welfare, and Other Public Associations	15,309	10,516	15,361	14,127
Hospitals, Sanitariums, Orphanages, Etc.	5,932	4,719	4,432	5,205
Schools and Colleges	6,012	5,516	6,257	5,101
Foundations	1,576	2,531	2,961	1,653
Total Institutions and Foundations	**48,264**	**39,028**	**44,176**	**42,075**
Other Institutional Investors Not Classified (a)	**41,383**	**45,062**	**244,187**	**305,421**
Total	**1,357,679**	**1,476,645**	**1,765,385**	**2,435,304**

(a) Includes institutional accounts which do not fall under other classifications and those for which no determination of classification can be made. Reporters of institutional data represented 80.9% of total accounts in 1984, 61.0% of total accounts in 1985, 53.3% of total accounts in 1986, and 50.4% of total accounts in 1987.

NOTE:

R – Revised

*Preliminary

Number of Accounts of Fiduciary, Business, and Institutional Investors In Money Market Funds by Type of Fund

	General Purpose		Broker/Dealer		Institutional	
	1986R	1987*	1986R	1987*	1986	1987*
Fiduciaries (Banks and Individuals Serving as Trustees, Guardians, and Administrators)	338,572	361,951	382,439	900,362	78,836	94,019
Business Corporations	124,919	125,267	141,908	131,222	6,589	7,670
Retirement Plans	157,187	217,895	211,609	211,693	5,507	3,274
Insurance Companies and Other Financial Institutions	11,890	9,537	11,330	14,193	2,393	676
Unions	139	741	3,687	9,286	17	22
Total Business Organizations	294,135	353,440	368,534	366,394	14,506	11,642
Churches and Religious Organizations	7,633	9,629	7,316	6,133	216	227
Fraternal, Welfare, and Other Public Associations	8,777	7,615	6,353	5,854	231	658
Hospitals, Sanitariums, Orphanages, Etc.	2,049	2,033	2,281	2,933	102	239
Schools and Colleges	2,354	2,198	3,789	2,737	114	166
Foundations	849	1,148	2,097	491	15	14
Total Institutions and Foundations	21,662	22,623	21,836	18,148	678	1,304
Other Institutional Investors Not Classified (a)	31,359	37,086	211,248	267,892	1,580	443
Total	685,728	775,100	984,057	1,552,796	95,600	107,408

(a) Includes institutional accounts which do not fall under other classifications and those for which no determination of classification can be made.

*Preliminary

R—Revised

Number of Accounts of Fiduciary, Business, and Institutional Investors In Short-Term Municipal Bond Funds

	1984	1985	1986	1987*
Fiduciaries (Banks and Individuals Serving as Trustees, Guardians, and Administrators)	**18,361R**	**35,585**	**49,196**	**85,683**
Business Corporations	3,952R	5,629	10,630	9,748
Retirement Plans	1,082R	121	523	2,218
Insurance Companies and Other Financial Institutions	4,215R	1,092	2,141	1,028
Unions	7R	7	4	527
Total Business Organizations	**9,256R**	**6,849**	**13,298**	**13,521**
Churches and Religious Organizations	15R	13	26	29
Fraternal, Welfare, and Other Public Associations	30	33	84	649
Hospitals, Sanitariums, Orphanages, Etc.	28	34	41	26
Schools and Colleges	67	17	41	56
Foundations	1	2	4	12
Total Institutions and Foundations	**141R**	**99**	**196**	**772**
Other Institutional Investors Not Classified (a)	**627R**	**1,528**	**6,262**	**3,969**
Total	**28,385R**	**44,061**	**68,952**	**103,945**

(a) Includes institutional accounts which do not fall under other classifications and those for which no determination of classification can be made.

NOTE: Short-term municipal bond fund reporters represented 89.7% of total accounts in 1984, 59.7% in 1985, 57.9% in 1986, and 61.9% in 1987.

R – Revised

*Preliminary

Assets of Fiduciary, Business, and Institutional Investors In Equity, Bond, and Income Funds

(Millions of Dollars)

	1984R	1985	1986	1987*
Fiduciaries (Banks and Individuals Serving as Trustees, Guardians, and Administrators)	**$12,877.8**	**$22,659.0**	**$51,076.1**	**$ 52,734.6**
Business Corporations	6,049.0	10,807.5	15,675.8	12,875.7
Retirement Plans	8,719.5	19,050.8	26,431.6	28,900.8
Insurance Companies and Other Financial Institutions	1,283.5	4,049.4	14,460.1	14,800.7
Unions	37.7	72.4	202.7	375.4
Total Business Organizations	**$16,089.7**	**$33,980.1**	**$ 56,770.2**	**$ 56,952.6**
Churches and Religious Organizations	336.2	593.8	853.6	1,428.9
Fraternal, Welfare, and Other Public Associations	303.5	477.3	1,186.9	994.8
Hospitals, Sanitariums, Orphanages, Etc.	136.7	267.9	497.7	466.7
Schools and Colleges	244.3	376.1	705.7	861.4
Foundations	81.8	265.8	467.7	749.1
Total Institutions and Foundations	**$ 1,102.5**	**$ 1,980.9**	**$ 3,711.5**	**$ 4,501.0**
Other Institutional Investors Not Classified (a)	**$ 2,672.9**	**$ 3,250.3**	**$ 5,407.1**	**$ 7,537.0**
Total	**$32,742.9**	**$61,870.3**	**$116,964.9**	**$121,725.2**

(a) Includes institutional accounts which do not fall under other classifications and those for which no determination of classification can be made.

NOTE: Reporters of institutional data represented 90.3% of total net assets in 1984, 85.0% in 1985, 84.7% in 1986, and 71.4% in 1987.

R—Revised

*Preliminary

Assets of Fiduciary, Business, and Institutional Investors in Money Market Funds

(Millions of Dollars)

	1984	1985	1986	1987*
Fiduciaries (Banks and Individuals Serving as Trustees, Guardians, and Administrators)	$60,809.3	$52,455.8	$ 61,292.4	$ 81,664.9
Business Corporations	16,062.0	12,817.4	14,230.7	14,348.7
Retirement Plans	8,099.2	9,078.3	13,116.2	11,757.4
Insurance Companies and Other Financial Institutions	6,993.7	7,396.7	7,548.7	6,523.8
Unions	137.1	81.8	514.6	606.6
Total Business Organizations	**$31,292.0**	**$29,374.2**	**$ 35,410.2**	**$ 33,236.5**
Churches and Religious Organizations	559.2	540.1	537.6	534.7
Fraternal, Welfare, and Other Public Associations	700.5	377.6	749.2	986.0
Hospitals, Sanitariums, Orphanages, Etc.	611.4	444.8	369.8	455.5
Schools and Colleges	444.2	291.2	431.3	498.4
Foundations	68.5	278.9	222.7	73.0
Total Institutions and Foundations	**$ 2,383.8**	**$ 1,932.6**	**$ 2,310.6**	**$ 2,547.6**
Other Institutional Investors Not Classified (a)	**$ 1,127.7**	**$ 5,939.5**	**$ 4,222.5**	**$ 6,076.2**
Total	**$95,612.8**	**$89,702.1**	**$103,235.7**	**$123,525.2**

(a) Includes institutional accounts which do not fall under other classifications and those for which no determination of classification can be made.

NOTE: Reporters of institutional data represented 78.8% of net assets in 1984, 62.4% in 1985, 53.3% in 1986, and 52.4% in 1987.

*Preliminary

Assets of Fiduciary, Business, and Institutional Investors In Money Market Funds by Type of Fund

(Millions of Dollars)

	General Purpose		Broker/Dealer		Institutional	
	1986R	1987*	1986R	1987*	1986R	1987*
Fiduciaries (Banks and Individuals Serving as Trustees, Guardians, and Administrators)	$ 9,543.1	$11,913.5	$ 5,842.3	$ 8,023.4	$45,907.0	$61,727.9
Business Corporations	5,850.3	5,952.0	5,648.8	5,146.2	2,731.7	3,250.5
Retirement Plans	4,558.2	6,465.2	7,179.7	5,017.3	1,378.2	274.8
Insurance Companies and Other Financial Institutions	3,378.7	3,961.1	1,252.1	958.6	2,917.8	1,604.1
Unions	368.4	81.6	142.6	507.6	3.6	17.4
Total Business Organizations	$14,155.6	$16,459.9	$14,223.2	$11,629.7	$ 7,031.3	$ 5,146.8
Churches and Religious Organizations	223.1	255.5	255.3	249.2	59.2	30.0
Fraternal, Welfare, and Other Public Associations	304.2	457.3	277.3	251.6	167.8	277.1
Hospitals, Sanitariums, Orphanages, Etc.	100.0	149.0	160.9	161.4	98.9	145.1
Schools and Colleges	153.4	111.6	170.3	305.1	107.6	81.7
Foundations	62.2	57.0	159.5	14.3	1.0	1.7
Total Institutions and Foundations	$ 852.9	$ 1,030.4	$ 1,023.3	$ 981.6	$ 434.5	$ 535.6
Other Institutional Investors Not Classified (a)	$ 1,048.3	$ 1,426.8	$ 3,099.4	$ 4,496.9	$ 74.9	$ 152.6
Total	$25,599.9	$30,830.6	$24,188.2	$25,131.6	$53,447.7	$67,562.9

(a) Includes institutional assets which do not fall under other classifications and those for which no determination of classification can be made.

*Preliminary

R – Revised

103

Assets of Fiduciary, Business, and Institutional Investors In Short-Term Municipal Bond Funds

(Millions of Dollars)

	1984R	1985	1986	1987*
Fiduciaries (Banks and Individuals Serving as Trustees, Guardians, and Administrators)	$ 7,452.4	$12,518.0	$25,549.5	$21,882.0
Business Corporations	1,144.2	1,702.6	3,891.3	3,091.8
Retirement Plans	52.6	8.0	127.2	106.6
Insurance Companies and Other Financial Institutions	1,736.0	1,576.8	2,465.6	656.4
Unions	0.3	0.2	25.5	229.0
Total Business Organizations	$ 2,933.1	$ 3,287.6	$ 6,509.6	$ 4,083.8
Churches and Religious Organizations	0.2	0.7	12.7	2.1
Fraternal, Welfare, and Other Public Associations	0.9	2.3	14.3	73.1
Hospitals, Sanitariums, Orphanages, Etc.	1.0	1.1	2.9	1.6
Schools and Colleges	2.5	5.2	2.7	11.5
Foundations	0.1	0.0	0.1	0.1
Total Institutions and Foundations	$ 4.7	$ 9.3	$ 32.7	$ 88.4
Other Institutional Investors Not Classified (a)	$ 166.5	$ 727.6	$ 572.6	$ 756.3
Total	$10,556.7	$16,542.5	$32,664.4	$26,810.5

(a) Includes institutional accounts which do not fall under other classifications and those for which no determination of classification can be made.

NOTE: Short-term municipal bond fund reporters represented 89.7% of total net assets in 1984, 65.5% in 1985, 61.5% in 1986, and 57.0% in 1987.

R—Revised

*Preliminary

Assets of Major Institutions and Financial Intermediaries
(Millions of Dollars)

	1982	1983	1984	1985	1986	1987
Savings Institutions						
Commercial Banks	$1,972,100	$2,093,800	$2,264,800	$2,483,800R	$2,597,700R	$2,721,400
Credit Union (a)	69,585	81,961	93,036	118,010	166,100	183,600
Mutual Savings Banks	174,197	193,535	203,898	216,776R	239,200	259,300
Savings & Loan Associations	707,646	838,386e	1,002,047e	1,080,649e	1,155,600R	1,263,300
Insurance						
Fire & Casualty (f)	$ NA	$ 225,300R	$ 241,000R	$ 289,900R	$ 346,400	386,800
Life	588,163	654,948	722,979	825,901R	905,900	1,006,900
Investment Institutions						
Bank Administered Trusts (b)	$ 689,040	$ 762,800	NA	NA	NA	NA
Closed-End Investment						
Companies (g)	NA	NA	$ 6,361	$ 7,581	$ 13,895	$ 20,492
Mutual Funds (c)	296,600	292,985	370,680	495,498	716,308	769,900

a – Includes only federal or federally insured state credit unions serving natural persons.
b – Reflects only discretionary trusts and agencies.
c – Includes Short-Term Funds.
d – As of November 1986.
e – Includes FSLIC insured institutions.
f – Federal Reserve Board, Flow of Funds Accounts.
g – Lipper Analytical Services, Inc.
NA – Not available
R – Revised

Index